Smile for a Change

How the World's Favorite Expression
Can Affect Your Life

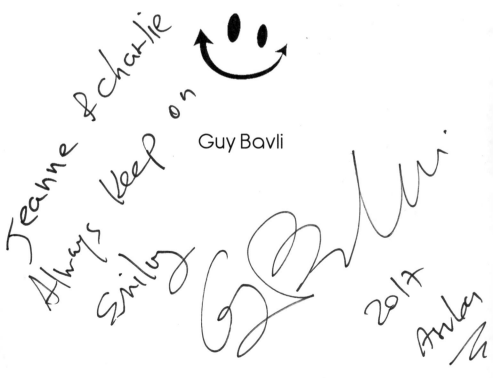

Guy Bavli

Jeanne & charlie
Always keep on
Smiley
2017

Books may be purchased by contacting the publisher, MOTM Publishing, Ft. Lauderdale, FL (USA) at 888.877.6463 or info@MasteroftheMind.com.

Published By: MOTM Publishing

Cover Design by: Jorge Cano
Interior Design by: Polgarus Studio
Cover Photography by: Munoz Studio Photography

Library of Congress Control Number: 2016913459
ISBN: 978-0-9979618-0-5
1. Book – Self-Help Techniques
 Printed in the United States of America

To learn more about Guy Bavli or sign up for newsletter, please visit:
www.MasteroftheMind.com

Follow us: @GuyBavli

Dedication:

I would like to dedicate this book in memory of my father: Shmuel Bavli.

He was a special person, an acquired taste. Not only was he a pilot, salt of the earth and man of the skys, but also a very funny man. He always had witty comments about everything in life that combined wisdom and humor.

One of his lines that I remember clearly was when I saw him talking to himself, moving his hands and nodding his head when no one else was around him. I asked him: *"Dad, why are you talking to yourself?"* and he would reply: *"I talk to myself because I like to talk to Smart People!"*

Dad, I love you and miss you, and your memory will always put a big Smile on my face.

This book is for you!

Contents

Forward

In my many years as a Comic, I have come to know the importance of laughter, but it wasn't until I read Guy Bavli's book that I realized the depth to which a smile can enhance our lives.

I first met Guy over twenty years ago, when he asked me to create and star in a comedy skit for his TV pilot. His positive persona convinced me to partake in what led to many years of friendship, laughter, and creation. He envisioned me playing a magician who fails at his tricks and succeeds only through error and pure luck. For me, this was an easy task since I had never done any magic before! My second memory of Guy involved even more laughter: in another slapstick sketch we did together, we played an engaged couple out shopping for a ring. My character, the woman, wanted a bigger ring than each one that was offered and Guy, bit by bit, bartered everything he had to get one—his watch, the shirt off his back, and finally even his pants—so that in the final scene, as I admired the huge sparkling rock on my finger, Guy was walking down the streets of Tel Aviv stripped down to nothing but his underwear! Then comedy spilled into real life as, on our way back from the shoot and still dressed for the sketch, the car broke down. We still laugh hysterically when we recall me in a dress pushing his terrible car uphill on a busy city street!

We went on to tour the country co-starring in the musical I wrote and directed, "The Sorcerer's Apprentice," and I have been privy to Guy's ever-ready, infectious smile ever since. I played the Sorcerer's Apprentice and Guy played the Sorcerer himself, which was an absurd reversal of real life since Guy is thirty years younger than me! Traveling and performing side by side solidified our friendship, and I realized we were both drawn to comedy for the same reason: the joy of making people feel good through laughter. Though he is now a brilliant mentalist, at the time Guy had an inexhaustible repertoire of comic magic sketches which he generously allowed me to perform. I was his Apprentice, so I could get away with doing them very badly... as long as I smiled! Luckily, this has never been a difficult thing to manage when around "Bubbly" Bavli.

Reading *Smile for a Change*, so thoroughly researched and offering so many insights on smiling, is like spending time with its author: you will be filled with new ideas and you won't be able to keep from smiling—but more importantly, you will understand what a smile can do for you!

Performing before audiences worldwide, I have learned that laughter is a universal healing element... and that before people cackle, titter, giggle, or roar with amusement, they *always* begin with a Smile. There is something magical in transforming people's expectations (what I imagine as the audience thinking, "Okay Clever Clogs, just try and make me laugh!") into a genuine, robust expression of happiness. Like the laughter that it produces, my style of slapstick comedy transcends cultural and linguistic barriers. Guy's delightful and comprehensive survey investigates the nature of this universal act: why do we smile, and how do different smiles mean different things across the globe? What chemical reactions in our brains does smiling set off? Ultimately, he asks, what power does a smile have to change our lives? In all my years of spreading laughter through performances, I have seen how it can help people from all over the world forget their daily worries and the humdrum stress of our existence. Guy's book has taught me how we can take the great feeling of going to a comedy show and apply it to daily life.

Audience members frequently come up to me after a performance, saying the same thing: "Before the show I felt really tired, empty and depressed. I certainly didn't feel like laughing or even smiling, but now I feel energized and wonderful!"

On a personal level, I feel the amazingly powerful benefits through my practice of smiling meditation before every show. This simple breathing meditation consists of smiling on the in-breath and feeling joy and gratitude on the out-breath, which is one of many methods that Guy mentions in his book. The comedy that I bring to the stage emerges from a pure smiling place: spontaneous, happy, and natural. My smiling meditation brings me to this place every time I perform; reading this book will help you inhabit this place on an everyday basis.

My own experiences, and those of my friends who are

hospital clowns, prove beyond a doubt the healing properties of smiling and laughter. We say for good reason that laughter is the best medicine. What we tend to forget is that a smile can come from within. It starts with you, and good news—you are already on the right track by holding this book in your hands!

Guy's lifelong work as a mentalist and entertainer shows the power of the mind to produce real, positive outcomes in our lives. Here, he offers overwhelming evidence that a smile is much more than a series of facial muscles contracting. These pages will teach you not only why smiling is so important, but also how to develop your smile and to "Mimic what's missing in your life." Smiling is the best tool for stress management and the forging of human connections. It's amazing for our health, our confidence, our professional and personal lives... and thankfully, it's very contagious!

Guy's book shows us how mirroring the genuine smiles of others gives us the power to make authentic smiles come more naturally. As someone who has spent his life making people laugh, I cannot over-emphasize the importance of moving through life with a smile on your face. With *Smile for a Change*, we finally have a heartfelt and entertaining How-to Guide on the benefits and power of the smile.

I have been waiting over fifty years for a book like this one... lucky reader, you have it before you right now!

Julian Chagrin, comedian
ISRAEL 2016

Introduction

Smiling has got me through tough times and opened many doors in my personal and professional life. Since childhood I was interested in the power of the mind, super heroes, magicians, and mystifiers, and trained in front of the TV watching them in action. That intuition early in my life showed that the power of smile is something that is already in me and ready to be used. That's an immense power within each of us that can bring fruitful changes in the life of any person who is ready to discover the potential of the power of smile.

My name is Guy Bavli. Over the past 30 years, I have toured the world entertaining, training and educating companies and audiences about the power of the mind. My travels through more than 50 countries worldwide have allowed me to learn and explore the cultures of many continents, to observe the differences and commonalities of human body language—and the power of smile is obvious and undeniable in every corner of the world. I also have been fortunate enough to experience the empowering feeling that comes from being in front of hundreds, thousands and even millions of people on the most famous stages and TV studios of the world. I love to entertain and surprise, but more than anything I'm entertained and surprised by the abilities of the most powerful computer in the world—human mind. That's a place where everything that has ever happened to you and everything that is yet to come meets. That's where you become who you are—in your mind that manifests into the world through your every action and expression. When you get your mind smiling, the entire world is ready to return its smile back to you in many different forms of positivity.

I have enthusiastically researched and observed the mysteries of mind, followed the studies and experiments held by the scientific community related to mind and proving the power of smile. In this book I'm putting it all together with my personal experiences, knowledge and intuitive findings to present them to you in an easily understandable manner. This book hasn't been written just for fun, but you can read it for fun as well—and if you do so, I will be happy to see you smiling.

While using and observing the power of smiles, I didn't ask myself if that's just an illusion or a "real thing." I didn't have to ask myself or anyone else if smiles really have any power to make changes. I knew it. I can feel it and you can feel it as well. The question is... are you using this power that is sparkling within you? This book was written to help you to acknowledge, unlock and unleash the life-changing potential of every smile you feel, express and share with others. It's a self-help book that will help you to:

- acknowledge the power of smile learning about it from different angles,
- change different situations using the power of your own smile,
- invite professional success and loving relationships in your life,
- get experience to change your mindset making it more open to positivity,
- open up for real, authentic happiness and enjoy it with peace in your mind,
- learn how you can help others around you to improve their lives,
- make the world a better place to live.

It might sound too good to be true... Are we talking about such a simple act as smiling? Can a smile bring changes in any field of life and can this book show how YOU can do it? Yes! But be warned: keeping this book on the shelf or a table isn't going to bring life changes, except some small change in your home interior. It's not the book that makes the change, but you putting in action what you read in this book. I wish I could bring a smile on your face as soon as you get the book in your hands, but I can't bring you peace, love and success if you are not willing to open up for it.

If you have an open mind, this book will set you on that path as it answers these, and other, questions:

- How the attitude to such a simple act as smiling has changed through history?

- What happens in your brain when you're smiling?

- How mimicking can improve your interaction with others?

- Can you see the difference between real and fake smiles?

- How to get the desired results without suffering and stress?

- How to heal your relationships that have gone wrong?

- How to change the mood in the room full of people?

- How we can leave smiles for the future?

You will learn a bit of history and travel between cultures that are expressed through our smiles. You will discover your inner chemistry and the magic of facial expressions, and you will find the way from conscious to subconscious mind. Within the pages of this book you will meet classical painters and doctors from modern scientific labs, you will get to know Joe the Doctor and Joe the Baker, and you will meet me through my personal experiences. You will meet yourself and be encouraged to observe and experiment with your own abilities. What comes after you have finished the book depends only on you, but I hope me and all those Joes in *Smile for a Change* can make your journey at least a little bit easier, faster and more joyful.

All I want to ask you reading this book is: keep your mind open, try to experience what you read and create the described experiences for yourself. When you are reading this book let the seriousness, anxiety and self-denial go on vacation and just have fun with your own superpower of smiling.

A smile is a powerful thing, you are powerful being, and you can *Smile for a Change*.

Guy Bavli
FL, USA 2016

1

Sharing Smiles through History

"Life is short, so smile while you still have teeth."
–Anonymous

C an you picture a happy moment in your life where you didn't smile? We smile when feeling good—it's a reflexive response to positive emotions after all— and with smiles in pictures we want to immortalize happy days and positive feelings. We believe that smiling makes us look better in pictures. Smiling people seem friendly, benevolent, and open—just the type of people we want to see around us. This is something marketers learn very fast: the smile subconsciously makes a connection between people and opens the door to mutual trust.

If you are looking for someone to ask for directions when lost in a strange city, would you walk to the always optimistic

Goofy from Mickey Mouse cartoons or a smart, sarcastic Grumpy Cat from the depths of the internet? The answer is obvious. We might appreciate Grumpy Cat's always sarcastic attitude when it's a safe distance from us, but even acknowledging that Goofy might not know the right answer, we all would first try to approach him just because of his trusty smile. Smiles are truly magical when written in our faces. We don't even need to know a person—if we can just share and receive back a genuine smile, we know deep down that we are not threatened and there is a chance we could become friends or at least have a decent and friendly chat. A simple smile can make a huge difference in most places and situations, from business meetings to family dinners.

So you smile when you feel good, of course. Smiling is an expression of joy, pleasure, and satisfaction that you feel inside, but do you know that it works the other way around? Try it the next time something terrible takes place and see what happens. When you smile, you actually start feeling better. It is the strongest remedy you can make to feel better immediately. It doesn't matter who you are, what you do or what troubles you—a smile is the only remedy available to all of us, the only remedy that affects us instantly. If it wasn't so effective, I would just mention smiling here and there and not give it a whole book.

In fact, I want you to check the power of smile on yourself right now. Just do one very simple thing: put a smile on your face. As simple as that, draw your lips up across your face! Feel how your cheeks and your eyes get involved in this simple action. Notice how your face is changing from cold and neutral to warm, kind and friendly? Close your eyes and imagine your whole body absorbing this smile. Let that smile inside of you, body and soul—feel it! It's a truly enjoyable feeling. A calming, empowering and balancing feeling that comes from twitching a few tiny muscles. So, close your eyes now for a few seconds and simply enjoy the pleasantness a smile brings to you.

When you have opened your eyes, keep reading with the expression of smile on your face! It's normal if the smile fades out while you're reading—it just happens as you focus on the text rather than on your smile. Don't force it. Just allow the smile to come back to your face! Don't stress yourself out, just smile with ease and keep reading.

There is no doubt that smiling people are beautiful. Now, when you are reading this with a natural smile on your face, you are the most beautiful version of yourself who could read this book. You know it. Everyone knows that smiling people are beautiful. Everyone feels it. Everyone wants to get a smile, because we are made to be attracted to beauty and pleasure, so we seek for it in ourselves just as much as in others. When it comes to interpersonal communication, smiling is a lot more valuable than an expensive jewel, or stylish and perfectly fitting clothes, or even small talk. You've probably heard people saying that a smile is the best decoration for a face. More than that, it's not just a decoration, and you are not a Christmas tree that needs to be wrapped in lights to shine.

I've met a few homeless people who look a lot more likeable than half the people partying in V.I.P clubs in L.A. on a Friday night. Clothes, style, make-up, the size of your wallet or speed of your car... none of these things make you likeable or unlikeable. Not even the shape of your face or your body, the fact that there is a star in the Universe sharing your name or that your best friend is the governor's son. It's your smile that makes you likeable because it comes from inside of you, and a genuine smile carries positive emotional information without saying a word. When you fake one, people recognize it instantly. When your smile is honest though, people become infatuated with it. We all know this at least intuitively, but when it comes to action... Huh, in our actions there are more holes than in Swiss cheese. When I started to research the history of smiling, I soon noticed that's more than a cutesy turn of phrase, but the best metaphor for our actions.

Before touching a bit on the history of smiling and its heritage, I want to share with you a bit of my own history.

When I was a child I was very fat, in fact, obese to say the least. I was a joke to most of my peers. I was always that fat kid, even in kindergarten and in the first grade I was twice the size of my friends in class. I was often bullied, called names, cornered and belittled. What could I do, kids are at times cruel, and as an awkward giant among naughty dwarfs I simply got into middle of their games just because I was there. I felt like what was inside of me didn't show on the outside, and interaction with my peers sometimes appeared to be like trying to convince a polar bear that a coconut is white on the inside. So, they danced around the coconut not knowing that it should be broken to reveal the truth. I needed to show who I am on the inside in order to cover the outside.

I was a fan of the unknown: magic, mystery and mysticism, as well as theater and comedy. However, I only saw it on TV and wanted to be like them—people who surprise others, make them smile and wonder, but I did not have the tools to achieve it at a young age of 5–6.

I had two talents:

1. I was very outgoing and had a great sense of humor. Always loved to make jokes, imitate teachers and famous people and do magic tricks that I learned from a magic box.

2. I was very intuitive. I always had the right answer and quickly understood situations.

You might imagine me as a little, depressed, grumpy boy who was suppressed by the jokes and comments of others, standing in front of a mirror imagining that a pencil is a magic stick and hoping that by just waving my hand, I could destroy all these people who were mean to me, but that wasn't the truth. I understood that being fat would not change as fast as I wanted (the intuition kicked in quickly) but instead I could show my friends who I am from the inside. Luckily, I was a SMILING BOY. I always took things with ease, made jokes, had a happy face and positive attitude. Sometimes this protected me from getting bullied because girls thought I was cute and made faces at the boys who tried to humiliate me. I was loved by the good kids since I was happy, positive and smiling no matter what. For me this opened door to many new friendships and alliances at school. Smiling my way into my teen years, I became socially centered and accepted because I was cool—a happy person.

Since I can remember, smiling has gotten me through tough times and opened many doors in my personal and professional life. Using and observing the power of smiles around the world, one question after another popped into my mind. Digging for logical answers led me to this book, although, logic is often left aside when it comes to something as widespread as... for example, social standards. As I said previously—more holes than cheese! The history of smiling can't be described in the manner you could tell the history of wars, rising taxes or washing machines:

> In 200 B.C. the first human started to smile. In 1123, June 15th Joe the Doctor started a new movement called "Smiling World." On May 7th, 1779 the law of smiling came into force across the U.S.

Well, you won't find that kind of list anywhere because the history of smiling can't be told by plain facts and numbers. Nobody knows who the first one to crack a smile was and there is no law of smiling. The history of smiling is a story about social standards and collective development of sensibility. So where and how did it all begin?

The development of spoken language is also often considered the beginning of intelligent communication—exchanging information between people. Humans evolved around 2 million years ago, but they didn't have any articulate language to communicate, yet we wouldn't be here now if our ancestors didn't find a way to communicate. They simply would have killed each other or hid from each other in bushes, making breeding and reproduction impossible. I believe people started to smile before they could talk because our genuine smiles come from the heart, and there is no need for language or deep knowledge to realize that smiling has power. Babies are a clear proof of that: after being just a few days in the world they already start sharing smiles. At the beginning they don't yet know that their smiles are telling something and affecting their communication with others;, so, they do it purely from the heart. Later, they acknowledge the power of sounds that they make and start using body language to communicate with others around them. It's similar to what our primitive ancestors might have done: they made sounds and noises, and before starting to put sounds together in words, they used what was natural – expressions of our strongest feelings. They developed body language that mostly is triggered by rational impulse. Of course, their body language wasn't as complex as ours is today, because they didn't have the sensibility a modern man has, but still—that's where communication actually starts—with natural emotional displays.

So when and how did we start to smile and share smiles with others? Some theories claim we can learn about the beginnings of smiling from the animal world. Do they smile? Turns out that, yes, they do! Check online for pictures of smiling apes—they really do it in a similar manner as humans (and it looks funny enough to affect me, making me smile back). If we look at the development of modern man by following evolutionary theory and try to understand the origin of our behavior by analyzing the behavior of our ancestors in the animal world, we can see that humans have smiled since arriving in this world. If we ignore evolutionary theory, by looking at newborn babies we can come to the same conclusion—smiling is innate. It's been around since the beginning of humanity, it's been a part of us since we were born.

The truth is that in the long and complex history of civilization, smiling has only been seen as something especially appealing for just over a century. At least that's what historical artifacts tell us—from sculptures and paintings, written works and not very old social standards of what acceptable behavior was. People smiled and shared smiles in private, but smiling in public wasn't for everyone. You would guess that only rich and powerful people could have the permission to smile—the higher class have always had more rights than anyone else. They make rules for others, raise peacocks in their gardens and ride unicorns—at least that's how privileged the higher class looks through the windows of homes of lower and middle class people. When it comes to smiling, it's a little bit different story... Smiling individuals weren't perceived as respectable and well-behaved people—it didn't matter for lower class, but was a rule of ethics for higher class (who looks more privileged now?). That was still the social standard until just a few centuries ago!

The biggest values back then were power, control and strength. It included also being educated and well-bred, but nothing about love, happiness, friendship or personal freedom. Powerful members of the public and those in higher positions than "ordinary people" had to be serious, otherwise they wouldn't be taken seriously. In a fearful and unaware society, seriousness could create the aura of being unbeatable and firm around you, making others scared and submissive—that was a perfect tool (and still is used as that) for building ruler-inferior types of relationships. In the 15th century, people couldn't even imagine that by 21st century, all respectable people would be smiling in hundreds of pictures without being perceived as foolish or frivolous. That thought might have been really insane! But here we are—now this is our reality. I would say, I'm glad to experience it.

If we look at classical Western art, we rarely see smiles. Medieval religious art doesn't depict smiles at all. The goddess of love has almost no expression in her face in famous painting, "The Birth of Venus" by Sandro Botticelli (15th century). There are plenty of paintings depicting women holding babies, but you can rarely find a smiling woman between them. You also don't see paintings of smiling kings and queens, knights or religious figures. Probably the first famous painting depicting a smile that comes to mind is Leonardo Da Vinci's "Mona Lisa" from 16th century. Her smile still grabs our attention and keeps revealing secrets as art historians and scientists continue to research this piece of art. Leonardo Da Vinci (1452–1519) wasn't just a painter. He also was a thinker, engineer, mathematician, musician, architect, botanist and more. For the late 15th and early 16th centuries, he was truly a man ahead of his time, and it almost seems that he had some secret knowledge that allowed him to create a simple, but magically appealing portrait of a woman with enigmatic smirk. I'm not an art historian, but I would guess that Da Vinci predicted the power of smile and wanted to embed it slowly into our evolution, hiding it behind a clever facial architectural mimic. It indeed came true to be the future power of communication.

While there are portraits with smirks and very shy smiles (usually depicting people who didn't care much for looking clever in their portraits), in classical art you don't often see a wide smile, especially a smile that reveals teeth. In Western culture until the 19th century, a smile that revealed teeth in art and life was strictly considered a feature of plebeians, poor people, children and frivolous characters like jokers, entertainers, artists, musicians, but never for serious men of influence. Not just in Europe, but also in Asia, a smile for a long time was perceived as a sign of foolishness and irrational behavior. For upper class etiquette required teeth to be covered with lips. It doesn't mean that people didn't smile for centuries, but art wasn't for depicting realities like public behavior. Art didn't reveal the truth and personalities of people but rather an ideal and status. I can imagine how hard it would be for me now to walk without a smile for even a few hours when I'm surrounded by others. After a few torturing hours, I would probably have to run to the mirror to check if that's still me and hysterically smile at my own reflection to make sure I'm still alive. Who knows, maybe the bold and the beautiful in medieval times did the same. We can only guess...

The first photo cameras in the Victorian era didn't fix many smiles either. It took about 15 minutes of posing to get a picture—try to keep a good looking smile for such long time! Try keeping a fake smile for just a few minutes as if you were posing for a picture! Your cheeks will start hurting pretty soon and I'm sure without training you won't be able to keep it 15 minutes later. So, back then smiling in pictures wasn't really possible and it was too expensive to damage the image with an unfortunate smile. To a modern man, family pictures and portraits from the beginnings of photography art seem pretty depressive and definitely very formal, not as we love to see them nowadays—joyful and filled with positive vibes.

Times changed and smiles became more acceptable.

Across many cultures today, smiling when someone is taking a picture is a reflex that we have gained with the development of photography and, as some theories claim, also dentistry. Until the 19th century, oral hygiene and dentistry was still far from good. The solution to every dental issue (basically, there was just one issue—pain) was pulling the aching tooth out. If half of your teeth are lost, showing them might be perceived as revealing your weakness, and demonstrating poor dental care would make you less appealing or simply might feel uncomfortable if it's going to be eternalized in a picture.

The end of the 19th century also brought us the cinema—moving pictures, but captured without sound. Sound couldn't be recorded together with the picture, but stories had to be told. Every intelligent being tells and perceives every story not just by words and actions. We also need emotionality. So, how could you show surprise, joy and happiness without words? Of course, by facial expressions, and when it comes to silent films, those expressions had to be magnified and exaggerated. One of my few childhood heroes was (and still is) Charlie Chaplin—magnificent actor in silent movies, the greatest non-verbal communicator who could tell stories and make us laugh without saying a word. You could understand all and more just by seeing him and his face, in particular. It's amazing how he could manipulate the viewer by his ability to mimic! For that, he will always remain a central figure of the era of silent films—the period in modern history that gave us permission to show our emotions and share smiles.

But the real game-changer was social development:

standards loosened and ways of self-presentation changed, as did attitudes to such a simple and natural feature as smile changed. The late 19th century allowed people to have more freedom in expressing themselves, and smiles finally became associated with beauty. Although many influential people were still holding on to the old standard of presenting themselves with a great dose of seriousness, society in general got the freedom to use their facial expressions in public without being seen as rude or light-headed.

By referring to what we know about smiling through the historical labyrinth of humanity's development, we can already announce that the 21st century is the century of smiles (and I'm not afraid to say it out loud with a truly happy smile on my face). This is era of taking selfies, smiling at yourself in mirrors and sharing smiles on streets and via social media. We don't know what the future will bring, but we can be sure that we have never been so free to smile as we are now.

Or maybe we aren't?

Maybe we still don't fully acknowledge the power within our smiles.

This is going to change. In fact, it's changing right now while you are reading this book and smiling or reminding yourself to smile. The change starts with you and I hope when you reach the end of this book, you will be free and empowered to use what you already have—your smile.

Civilization and society are constantly growing and developing. We are discovering more and more about ourselves as we learn about our needs and capabilities. A caveman was driven by many instincts we have partly lost nowadays, but he didn't have the sensibility a modern man has. A medieval man didn't have the same perception we have now. I'm pretty glad the progress has brought to us not just advanced technologies, but also better understanding of ourselves. Now we are finally aware of the mind–body connection more than ever: self-awareness is a trend, and frankly, the essence. People know that we need to reprogram ourselves to feel better, look better and live a quality life. We as humans are still a mystery with many things to solve, but we sure feel freer to express ourselves and show what we feel. Emotional displays in our faces are like pictures worth thousands of words. Especially in our times when evil is threatening to take control, there is no better time than now to smile, share that special energy and spread the positivity—one smile at a time.

With the development of technology we have amazing opportunities to travel around the world, which promotes mixing cultures and traditions, learning from each other much faster. A smile is an essential part of non-verbal communication in every corner of the world, but in some situations, it's not used the same way everywhere. A sign of happiness and positive emotions? Yes, but not just that. It turns out that behind our smiles, there aren't always corresponding emotions and feelings. Smiles can have different meanings, and there is something special that happens in the human brain behind our smiles... You already noticed it when I asked you to smile reading this chapter, right? Subconsciously, you already know that there is something beneficial and healing in your own smile. My plan is to give you more information so that even the most doubtful, logical mind will see smiling in a new light, to help you understand, accept and approve your smile and be able to access its power every minute of your life. That, and more, is what this book is about.

2

Cultural Smiles around the World

"A warm smile is the universal language of kindness."
– William Arthur Ward, American author and poet

W e don't smile just because we feel good, but we definitely feel something every time we smile. In previous centuries it hasn't been easy to research smiling due to lack of understanding and tools, but gaining collective experience and due to the development of research methods, we are moving forwards and discovering what stands behind a smile. The veil of magic slowly disappears as we get explanations to many things we couldn't explain previously. We know that the Earth has a round shape and it spins around the Sun. We have measured that our noses can recognize about 50 000 different scents, and we know that Donald Duck comics were banned in Finland in 1970s because the duck doesn't wear pants. Do we know everything about smiling now? We surely feel many things, but sometimes logic gets trapped in feelings we can't explain, although they are real. We don't know it all yet, but it doesn't mean we shouldn't talk about what we know, and science has proved this.

Step by step, our common knowledge is developed and we move closer to understanding ourselves. Depending on where you live in the world, your smile and other emotional displays are sending out and making perceivable not just personal messages but information about your cultural heritage as well. Before learning about the physical aspects of smiling, we first need to discuss cultural backgrounds that are projected in our smiles.

I can't imagine any corner of the world where smiles aren't shared, but I wanted to answer the question whether the meaning behind a smile is the same everywhere in the world. Generally, as an expression of happiness, a smile really works everywhere the same way, but in some situations, you can spot differences of expressing smiles depending on the cultural background of a person.

Universality of Emotional Displays

Trying to discover the full picture of human evolution and behavior famous English biologist, naturalist, geologist and scientist Charles Darwin (1809–1882) established the idea of the universality of emotion expressions in the 19th century. He hypothesized that everywhere around the world people use the same facial expressions to show basic emotional states: happiness, fear, anger, sadness, disgust and surprise. He held on to the idea that our basic emotional displays are universal—the same everywhere around the world. Darwin concluded that the basic emotional states are a heritage people in every corner of the world inherited from a single source—the first humans (assuming that we all come from the same first human beings). This means that facial expressions of basic emotions aren't learned and developed due to cultural background, but rather they are biologically innate and universal.

Darwin's conclusions were accepted by the scientific community, and many other studies of emotional expressions have been conducted based on Darwin's idea. The most notable researcher in this field is Dr. Paul Ekman, who maintains that the most universal emotional displays around the world exist in five categories: anger, fear, disgust, sadness, and enjoyment.[1] Actually, Pixar-Disney's animation film "Inside Out" (2015) shows how these five basic emotional states work in a clear and easily understandable fun way. The animation film tells a story of a young girl (Riley) and her emotions as she grows up and moves to another city together with her parents before hitting her teenage years. In this film, you see her actions and reactions and you also get inside the head of a girl where five basic emotions—joy, fear, sadness, anger and disgust—are depicted as human-like colorful characters interacting and trying to do their best to make Riley's life better. You see how these emotions interact. You get a glimpse into the mysterious ways of how human memory works and dreams are made, and you can also learn about the little voices inside yourself—your own emotions. It's not a documentary where everything is in accord with latest findings in neuroscience, but it gives a pretty good insight into our own emotional worlds. It's definitely not just a film for kids!

There is a little problem with the universality of emotional displays... Emotional states might be innate and similar to someone on the other side of the world, but are we absolutely powerless to our emotions and do we always display the same emotional expressions in the same situations? We all have a wide range of emotions, and we aren't just machines that run purely on biologically installed programs. We are not robots. We actually learn to use and control our innate, natural abilities, and this is not a process that only happens on a personal level without being affected by the culture and environment we live in.

We all are born with a reflex and natural ability to smile when there is a trigger for smiling (we will talk more about it in the next chapter). Even newborn babies smile before they could have consciously learned it. Their first way to communicate their needs is through facial expressions of happiness and sadness. Blind people smile although they've never seen anyone smiling—it definitely is an innate expression of happiness, but we learn showing, controlling and hiding our emotions, and it doesn't happen exactly the same way everywhere around the world.

In 2010 Rachel Jack at the University of Glasgow (UK) conducted research that challenged the idea of the universality of emotional expressions.[2] One of Jack's main arguments was that the majority of previously conducted studies of the universality of emotional expressions were based on Western European culture, but conclusions were drawn about people in the entire world. If those basic expressions are universal it means that people everywhere around the world should recognize them as expressions that carry the same emotional information. So, for the study she invited two different groups of participants: Western Caucasians and East Asians who hadn't spent much time around Westerners. The participants had to look at facial expressions on two faces—Western Caucasian and East Asian—that were created on a computer. Seeing the faces, participants could choose which of the basic emotions are expressed and even rate the intensity of emotions. If all participants (regardless of their cultural background) recognized the same emotions in the same faces, the theory of universality of emotional displays would be proven, but that isn't what happened. Westerners easily matched faces with Darwin's basic emotional states, but East Asians saw faces differently. Through this experiment Rachel Jack actually proved that we do not have the same emotions behind the same facial expressions everywhere around the world – they are affected and developed by social cues from the culture we live in.

Cultural Differences in Our Smiles

You know that humor sometimes can be funny in one place but get no response or even upset someone in another place. Interpreters know this issue very well. They also know that the best way to make the audience give a foreign speaker the desired response is in place of translating a joke, just saying: "The speaker just made a joke. Please laugh." It's because humor sometimes isn't translatable because of the specificities of culture or language, but sometimes it's simply inappropriate because of the way of that thinking differs depending on where you come from.

Throughout my many travels around the world, I had to accommodate my show to fit the sense of humor and cultural understandings of people I was going to talk to. A joke that works in one place doesn't always work in another. In fact, it might offend some people and turn out sad not funny. So if my plan was to visit an exotic country that I never visited before, I usually came 1–2 days early and went out to the markets to look at people. Markets for me were always the best places to get to know cultural backgrounds and understandings because that's where you see people and merge with the culture. I spoke with as many people as I could to learn about their culture and humor, and I even tried different jokes and one-liners to see what makes them laugh and what doesn't have an effect. Do they react to my body language, and if so, in which way? Do they react to English language humor? If I had a translator with me, I would take him/her for few hours and see if my humor translates well via a translator. This gave me an understanding of their humor and how to adjust my presentation to fit the audience's cultural background.

Humor sometimes doesn't get perceived the same way everywhere just as shared smiles may be perceived differently. The entire world smiles, and while happiness and joyfulness are expressed with a smile everywhere around the world, people with different cultural backgrounds can send different information with the same facial expressions. I think the easiest way to explain and understand this is by comparing Asian and Western cultures—that's where we can easily see these differences and contrasts.

First, while reading smiles, Westerners pay more attention to the lips while Asians focus more on the information given by eyes. It's not that one of these facial features is more important than other—they both send emotional messages to the world. What makes the difference is how we use our faces to express emotions and what emotional displays we are used to seeing.

When I performed in India for the first time, I was really confused. People were extremely nice, always friendly and smiling, which made me feel warmly welcome. However, each time I asked them for something, they would smile while bobbing their head left to right as saying NO. At first I didn't understand what they meant, so I asked again, and they replied by repeating the same gesture: smiling while bobbing their heads as if to say NO. I was baffled. Why were they smiling at me while at the same time shaking heads "NO"? I then asked someone and he told me: "No, no, no… When we agree, we nod our heads from left to right!" I told him in our gestures, YES means UP and DOWN, and NO means LEFT to RIGHT. He then nodded his head again from left to right, smiled and said: "Yes, I know!" It was extremely confusing and funny for me to see this difference—how one obvious expression of body language we think of as universal, can be exactly the opposite in another country!

The following might sound like a beginning of a cultural joke, but it's not. If a Japanese who has never met anyone from

Europe meets a Frenchman who has always lived in a traditional French environment, they both would have many surprises and misunderstandings because it would be hard for both of them to read each other's emotional expressions. But if the same Frenchman had lived in Japan for a few years or had spent a lot of time with a Japanese community in France, he would have learned the gestures Japanese people use to express emotions and communicate in a way that would make him understandable to Japanese as well.

Unconsciously we adjust our emotional expressions to the society we are in and to people we spend time with, but it doesn't happen immediately when we meet someone from a different cultural background. It takes time, because before adjusting and accommodating oneself with different expressions, we have to learn them. Sometimes we learn by understanding and accepting, but most of the time, by mimicking. When we mimic others it happens unconsciously in order to show that we accept and understand – to show that we have something in common. It's called mirroring & matching—that's something humans do when they are together. The main question is who is mirroring whom, which we'll delve into further in Chapter 5, "The Magic of Mimicking."

Cultural differences are reflected in our smiles because we use smiles depending on what is socially acceptable in different situations. We learn to control our emotions according to situations—if something seems funny in one situation, you would laugh out loud, while in another one, just a short smirk would appear on your face for a brief period.

Compared to Western cultures, emotional display in Asia

is more suppressed than accepted and encouraged. For example, in Korea a smile can create doubts about your credibility and intentions. Of course it doesn't apply to kids—those unrefined jewels who are still growing and learning the basics of living in their surroundings. Koreans are kind and welcoming people, but most likely you won't receive a wide open American smile—they just don't show their emotions like that. On the other hand, if you receive a very big American smile anywhere in the world including U.S., no one can guarantee that it is always a 100% genuine smile. They want you to feel welcome, so by smiling they are trying to make you feel more comfortable. They were trained to smile this way when they were hired for any job, and their culture teaches them to welcome others kindly. Between us, better a fake smile than genuine anger!

I was fortunate to visit South Korea a few times for TV appearances and other presentations. Koreans are very kindhearted and warm people, yet very proud as well, and their privacy and space is important. Their smile is small, but still serves as a way of greeting. However, when they are surprised or happy, they show a broad clear smile, leaving no doubt in your mind that they are happy!

Another example is China: for the 2008 Olympics in Beijing, volunteers who workers actually had to learn how to smile in way that would make them look friendly to Western visitors and TV viewers around the world. Thousands of people learning to smile "the way Westerners do it"—it sounds even a bit scary, like Westerners weren't able to accept Eastern hospitality if it weren't presented the "the right way". Well, they really did a good job and they truly looked joyous. When Westerners go to Asia for business, they learn to do things Asian way for similar reasons. And isn't that beautiful that we are so different, yet so much alike? Can you imagine a world where everyone looked and acted the same? I believe I'm not the only one who appreciates differences between cultures and our amazing opportunities to be friends, share love and learn from each other.

In many countries, unwarranted smiling can be perceived as "smile on duty" or fake smiling. This doesn't create a good impression of a person—for example, in Russia. Politeness is important, but smiling isn't a necessary part of being polite in Russia, and doing so can be perceived as bad taste. Fake smiling could also create a cold impression of yourself and send the signal that you are being dishonest and hiding your real emotions. In Russia, smiles are shared between people who are close to each other, while smiling at strangers, on the other hand, can be considered simply awkward. For an American it might seem that Russians smile less, but that's not necessarily the case: Russians simply need an obvious reason to smile. Just like in America, smiling in Russia is used as an expression of happiness and enjoyment, but for Americans it also is a sign of confidence. Meanwhile in Russia confidence still goes hand in hand with seriousness (and the correct answer to 1+1 seems to be the one the government has approved of, depending on the weather).

In many Asian countries, a smile can be a sign of embarrassment, confusion, fear, resignation or discomfort, while at the same time being used to express positive emotions. Got a promotion? Smile! Got fired from job? Smile!

Can't keep your promise due to unexpected obstacles? Smile! Just saw Popeye the Sailor Man riding a giant butterfly and can't understand if what you actually saw was real? Smile! At the end it's not that bad of an idea! But how can you actually read what stands behind smiles? If you stare at your phone and don't pay attention to the person you are talking to, you really can't read what stands behind his or her facial expressions—you just don't see them to read them. So first pay attention. You can also try to read what stands behind the smile by remembering that in Western cultures, a smile is expressed more through the mouth while in Eastern cultures, the focus is on eyes. When interacting with others, you pay attention to the whole picture and see not just eyes or mouth, but everything together (including their gestures, posture, tone of voice etc.). If you are in touch with your human feelings, you will be able to successfully read the emotional displays of anyone.

A smile is always better than an empty face or a negative expression, especially when we want to open a door or make a positive first impression. No matter where you are from, people will greet you better if you are smiling! The fact is, despite the differences in heritage and culture, the modern world gives us the ability to communicate and share our faces and lives with each other. Though some only see and share things in their communities, we are still more open to the world and what is around us. In a way, this makes us more universal in our actions and more understanding of others' actions.

Even within the framework of the same cultural background, two different people might mean different things when they smile. Yet, if we have an open mind, meeting in person we manage to read the emotional information a smile brings because we have our senses. It might be useful to learn about different types of smiles as it could improve your communication and social interaction, but before that, there is still one urging question—what exactly happens to us when we smile?

3

Behind the Smile

"A smile is a curve that sets everything straight."
–Phyllis Diller, American comedian

A genuine smile brings a message that is perceivable and understandable. We don't smile just to comply with social and cultural standards. First, it's our expression of happiness and enjoyment—and that's the same everywhere around the world. The big question is what happens to us when we smile—why does smiling make us feel good? We often hear that we should smile more, but is there any reason or justification that clearly explains why we should do it? We feel many things, but it's always interesting to look "behind the curtain" and check what science says. In addition to providing you with ways to help to use your smile effectively, you will explore many benefits of smiling in this book. First, let's get through some basic physiology and psychology of smiling. I promise it won't be long and difficult! I just want to provide some informational food for your mind to help it process this information.

In, on and around our heads—that's where physiology, psychology, biology, culture and history come together. What makes the show good is the work put in it behind the curtains. What makes your face radiate when smiling is what happens behind the visible part of your body. A smile is like a doorbell or a light switch that starts a complex mechanism in our brains. It is also in the in-between of something/someone pushing the button and the response created in us.

You can show a big, shiny smile, smile just with your eyes or deep down in your heart—when you smile genuinely the feeling of happiness and satisfaction already is in you and it could simply be there without letting it appear on your face. But what creates this visual display of your emotions?

Facial Muscles in Action

To a cursory viewer it might seem that only muscles around the mouth are participating in creating a smile. Try to put a short, simple smile on your face! If you try it, you will see what I'm talking about. Experience will help you understand and acknowledge things more than just reading information. So put that short, simple smile on your face right now! Only your mouth works to push your cheeks up a little, right? That is, of course, a fake smile, but it still looks like a smile even though all you had to do was contract your lips to form it.

Now, think about something positive—remember the most beautiful moments of your wedding day or maybe the day you got divorced, if that's your day of victory. Imagine and visualize getting something you've been longing for—something overwhelmingly positive like winning the lottery, travelling around the world in a private yacht or getting two burgers for the price of one. Imagine whatever makes you happy, and let the positive emotions of satisfaction, enjoyment and happiness spread throughout your mind. Now, let this feeling project on your face as well—smile and charge this simple act with positive attitude and joy. How does it feel? Is that just your mouth that forms a smile now or are other muscles being used as well?

It's a popular belief that smiling requires less effort than frowning because it involves less facial muscles than frowning. Whoever made up the saying, "It takes more muscles to frown than it does to smile," may only have wanted to inspire lazy people. The truth is there is no clear answer to how many muscles are involved in smiling. We all might have the same number of bones, but we don't have the same number of facial muscles. The most popular number is 43, but researches prove that we can have additional muscles in our faces and the number of missing or additional muscles can be up to 19. There isn't really a clear answer to which involves more muscles: smiling or frowning, because it depends on how many muscles you have and how many you use for each expression.

If we take a short glimpse into human anatomy we can find out that in grimacing, 6 pairs of facial muscles are involved, or 12 muscles in total on both sides of a face, in addition to other muscles that aren't always the same for all of us. There is also the seventh cranial nerve or the so called "facial nerve," that participates in making grimaces, including your smile. This nerve is directly connected to your brain. It transfers the information from your tongue and controls the production of facial expressions.

When you smile genuinely, your facial muscles ensure that your smile involves the entire face, not just your mouth. As corners of the mouth are rising, your cheeks, jaw, nose and nostrils, eyelids, forehead and even your neck get involved into the process. Try once to check! It's like a full-face exercise! As facial exercises help tone our faces and live without puffy eyes and double chin and keeps us looking younger. Isn't that already a good reason to smile? Train your facial muscles more and you might even get into the book of Guinness World Records for lifting weights with your cheeks!

Smile Triggers

A smile isn't a purely physical action. So, what makes us engage our nerves and muscles to form a smile?

Before you form a smile, there has to be a trigger that makes you contract your face. There are two types of triggers: physical and psychological.

When you are tickled, you smile or even laugh as crazy, but that doesn't necessarily mean you feel happy about it— there is a fine line between enjoying tickles and feeling like you are being held hostage. You will smile because touch is a physical trigger.

Feeling tickles is a neurological response to light forms of touch, and in some body parts, it tickles more than in other body parts because of natural self-defense mechanisms. It tickles the most in those body parts that are usually protected and have more nerves. So, we learn to let only people close to us touch these places (feet, armpits or neck, or other body areas that are very ticklish). Have you ever wondered why almost everywhere on a child's body is ticklish, but for adults just some parts, and not always the same parts for all of us? Here is the answer—children are more sensitive and weaker than adults, but with experience and hardening, we learn to control how much we allow those light touches affect us.

And why are so many body areas ticklish when touched by someone else, but doesn't have the same reaction when we touch them on our own? Self-defense is the answer! We just know we won't harm ourselves. Being tickled by somebody else or tickling someone actually can be a great trust exercise between people, of course, we wouldn't let everyone do it. In fact, if you closed your eyes and focused on the tickled area when somebody else is tickling you, you could stop feeling tickles. It just requires some brain power.

So if tickles come from our self-defense mechanism, why do we smile if it makes us feeling threatened? Scientists suggest it might be because we learn this reaction to tickles soon after we are born. When it comes to smiling, it's pretty hard to divide which triggers are physical and which are psychological. Our thinking and psyche in general doesn't work separately from our physical bodies, yet it rules over our physical actions processing different kinds of information we receive and connecting it with information we already have. It's no big wonder that the human mind still is the most powerful and the most mysterious computer on Earth.

Would your smile be physiologically caused if you ate your favorite food? The answer is "yes" and "no" at the same time. If you were truly hungry and got food satisfying your primal physical needs, a smile might arise because of a purely physical reason, but if you get your favorite ice cream for dessert after a nice meal, the smile on your face appears because of the thought of getting what you wanted. When someone receives a diploma, he hasn't satisfied a primal physical need, yet he smiles because he knows he deserves it after having worked long and hard for it. When Joe the Baker gives flowers to his wife, she smiles not because she desperately needed the flowers, but because she feels appreciated and loved. When Joe the Doctor hears his son listening to Mozart's Symphony No.40, he starts smiling because he is proud of his son's choices and taste in music. It's about the satisfaction that comes from a thought. It's about psychological triggers.

Psychologically caused smiles come from the reward system in brain. In short, you know what to expect so you act according to your knowledge of how to get it. When you meet a childhood friend, you have made many beautiful memories together and you smile because you are expecting to have more good times together. We are attracted to pleasure and we seek for it because of the reward system in our brain. There is a collection of brain structures that make us reach out for satisfaction by regulating our behaviors. We have addictions, cravings and motivations because of this system.

Humanity can even thank its survival to this system as well.

We install in our minds different patterns that our thoughts follow, which in turn define our behavior. Those patterns or pathways are formed from our experiences and memories, influenced by what we learn from others and our social and cultural background. Those patterns can be learned with intent and later become habits that rule our behavior straight from the subconscious mind, but also we can act according to these patterns without ever becoming aware of them. (This is the reason why I want you to try everything written in this book and check it "on your own skin"—your brain patterns come from experience. You will get to know many exercises and experiments in this book, so, do not hesitate to really experience them.)

When we face any kind of enjoyment, it triggers a smile, and that's where chemistry comes in.

Chemistry in Your Brain

The first thing is a trigger that in no time gets processed in your mind. It happens so fast that you can't really follow it. Your brain is like a library that contains books you know very well, and those that you haven't even acknowledged. There are memories, experiences, literary knowledge, sensory information, innate reflexes and needs, conclusions you've made, influences, your own opinions and stories others have told you, your secret thoughts and wishes, and the list goes on. When the trigger comes, the brain connects it with information in your personal library, not just taking it from "books" that you like, but also from those that you would want to hide somewhere or don't even know exist in the deepest corners. You don't even feel that fast stroke of lightning that brings a smile to your face, but here it is—you're smiling. The button is pushed, the mechanism started.

Let's say you've inhaled nitrous oxide, known as laughing gas. You lose your balance, fall down and laugh in a euphoric state—for a minute. It isn't as fun as it sounds or might look. It's actually very hazardous and can be deadly, so don't try it. It's not an experience anyone needs. I'm mentioning it here just to explain how brain chemistry works. The small molecules of this chemical rush through your respiratory system and travel straight to your brain. When they reach the brain, these small molecules start interacting directly with and stimulating specific brain receptors that make you smile and laugh. What happens when you face a trigger that has nothing to do with brain-stimulating chemicals reaching your brain? The same thing: when you smile your inner chemist awakes in your brain and starts producing natural chemicals, making you feel better.

Smiling activates your brain, sending it the message, "Make me feel good now!" Then your brain starts producing and releasing so called "feel good chemicals" and adjusting your levels of hormones, neurotransmitters and so on.

The main names of "feel good chemicals" are endorphins, dopamine, oxytocin and even adrenaline, which can kick in to replenish the process. Endorphins are neurotransmitters; dopamine stimulates the reward system in your brain and can get you even to euphoric state; oxytocin plays a big role in developing trust and helping to relax. As levels of some feel good chemicals are raised, levels of some stress hormones, for example cortisol, are lowered. By the way, high cortisol levels are related to headaches, insomnia, tiredness, anxiety and gut issues. Lowering your cortisol levels alone is a good reason to smile. Just one smile can help in so many ways! Look from whichever angle you want—it's a win-win situation! We won't get deep into analyzing each of these feel good chemicals. Let's leave it to scientific research laboratories, but take a note here: the more you smile, the more positivity it creates into your mind and body. Injecting your body with positivity is the best healing mechanism.

When a smile appears on your face it sends new information to the brain, and your brain gets a signal to shut out negativity and start the wheel of positive emotions and triggers. You get into a circle of positivity that grows and feeds from itself, releasing more of those "feel good chemicals" that can quickly improve your mood. As science enthusiasts say, we don't need big cars, huge houses or flying carpets to be happy, all we need is just some natural daily chemistry into ourselves—and it's not about magical pills!

Looking at smiling from this angle, it becomes clear why some people smile in unpleasant situations instead of panicking. A smile can be a natural mechanism to keep control over negativity and stay balanced. That's exactly why smiles are often used in many Asian countries where cultural heritage promotes smiling in this manner. We don't smile just when we feel good, but we can also smile to start feeling better.

Thich Nhat Hanh (born on 1926) is a Vietnamese Buddhist monk, author, speaker, poet and spiritual leader who many people around the world call their teacher. He also speaks a lot about smiling and its importance. Thich Nhat Hahn started his journey of being a monk at the age of sixteen. He helped suffering people during the war in Vietnam, and in 1961, he travelled to the U.S., bringing with him the ideas of Buddhism to the Western world, teaching non-violence and compassion, peace and ways to inner transformation. He is the master of mindfulness who is still teaching, living in Plum Village—a large Buddhist monastery in France where everyone is welcome to learn mindfulness.

This experienced teacher often speaks about smiling because it heals, helping us to stop suffering and acknowledge the joy within ourselves. In his speeches and interviews, he often mentions smiling meditation. The simplest version of his smiling meditation is breathing in and smiling when exhaling. You don't have to feel joyful to smile, but you can smile to start feeling joyful, because there is a lot to be happy for—your eyes help you see, your ears ensure that you hear the beauty of music and voices, you can move, you are alive. Enjoying a cup of tea, feeling the warmth of the sun on your skin, even while brushing your teeth or doing the dishes, there's something to acknowledge and smile in thankfulness. There's an endless list of things to be happy for! It's easy to get trapped into suffering, stress and worries, but it's also easy to get out of that all if you smile.

Thich Nhat Hanh offers a very simple exercise that can be practiced by any person: mindful smiling while acknowledging the good in the moment here and now. Simply close your eyes, take a deep breath and smile when breathing out. You can smile while exhaling and be thankful for what you focus on in each moment—it can be your body parts that work well or little moments in your life you are able to experience and enjoy. If you wake up in the middle of the night, close your eyes, breathe in and smile while exhaling in thankfulness for being in the here and now. Before a fresh meal, simply smile for having it. It's about taking a pause to smile for what you have. Isn't it easy? To experience how the smile creates joy, simply share a smile with what you have, for example, the eyes that allow you to read here and now. Share a smile with what you have— with your emotions, with your experiences, with your own body parts, with things and obstacles inside of you and outside. Close your eyes, inhale and exhale, thinking of that one good thing here and now. Smile at that good thing while exhaling.

The physiology and chemistry of smiling has great healing power. It heals from inside and out and actually works like medicine in many fields of our lives – from physical issues to social interaction. It's an apple a day that keeps the doctor away. A smile a day will do more: it will heal you making the doctor your friend without asking him to solve your health issues.

4

Smile for Your Health

"It is almost impossible to smile on the outside without feeling better on the inside."
—Anonymous

I believe that a smile is a cure for many different aches—from purely physical to emotional ones, from small and recent to old and seemingly unsolvable ones. It has a strong potential to heal and transform you from the inside and out. It's like medicine for many issues. The good thing is that you don't have to search or pay for it. There might be no such thing as a free lunch without a hidden catch, but there is a free and fast medical aide without pills or doctors. You don't even have to dial a phone number or rub Aladdin's lamp to call for the force that can help. You already have that free, fast helper and it's patiently waiting to be used. The only thing you need to do is to use it. It's done by smiling.

Obviously, I'm not the only one who feels the healing powers of smiles and it's not just philosophers who are giving credit to smiles for making our lives better. Have you heard about Clown Care? It's a program that gets stronger and stronger around the world, involving specially trained clowns who cheer up kids at hospitals. Dr. Clown is slowly becoming a common character at absolutely normal, respectable hospitals. Clowns aren't just jokers anymore. Smiling's power is researched and acknowledged, not just at family gatherings but also among medical professionals.

Smiles make us feel better and positively affect our physical and mental health—using such phrases is no longer just a sign of an idealistic personal world view, but a fact. Thanks to feel good chemicals, smiling helps reduce pain and lower stress levels as good as quality sleep. It also boosts our immune systems, helping us avoid different illnesses and even adding some time to our lives. There are many big and small health benefits that smiling can bring into your life. It heals you on emotional and even interpersonal levels, but it doesn't mean your physical, material body is immune to this power. First, it heals your physical body.

• Smile to Stop Physical Pain

"Feel good chemicals" we talked about previously are there to make you feel good, not just mentally or emotionally, but physically as well. The smile triggers the production of feel good chemicals, which then switch off and on different parts and processes in your brain that regulate your entire body.

Physical pain can be reduced if you smile! The small, ordinary pains, like stubbing your toe, mistakenly hitting your finger with a hammer, or getting elbowed at a rock concert, can all be reduced and relieved if you keep a smile on your face. If you focus on pain when it hurts, the pain grows stronger, but if you are directing your attention to positivity and let out your smile, feel good chemicals will help you recover faster. If you are suffering from regular physical pain, try "smile therapy"—find something to laugh about or force yourself to laugh at for least 10 minutes.

Sometimes all you need to get rid of a headache is a glass of water; I guess everyone knows how important it is to stay hydrated. It's simple, right? And it works! Now, you can add to your medicine chest one more powerful, simple and easily usable painkiller—smiling. If you focus on positivity, laugh and smile, in many situations you could kiss painkillers goodbye.

Smile to Stop Stress and Relax

When your stress levels are rising, smiling is probably the last thing that comes to mind. Meditation or exercise are pretty good ways to reduce stress, but the reality of how we deal with stressful situations is often far from being truly beneficial. Some people reach for a cigarette to calm down; some search for unhealthy comfort foods; and others simply let the stress take over. It's probably time to change your ways of dealing with stress. All you need to reduce stress is the natural brain chemistry that's activated by smiling.

Feeling a simple smile on your face, in your mind and in your heart is a great relaxant as well. When mental and physical tension rises in your mind and body, the greatest help is relaxation. All those tensions simply need a release or they will take away your productivity, creativity, energy, peace and even a good night's sleep. The easiest self-help tip to relax: smile! It will release not just mental or emotional tension, but it also works as a physical muscle relaxant.

Sometimes it's not easy to stay positively minded, especially if your mood is suppressed under the burden of stress. In hypnosis, guided imagery and meditation, a person's attention has to be directed the right way. It's similar with staying positive: you need the door that will allow your mind go in the desired direction. When you put a smile on your face, it becomes a trigger that directs your attention to positivity instead of your troubles. It's like a happiness injection that works even in confusing moments. Sometimes we simply need to trick our psyche into feeling better. The subconscious mind is gullible; it doesn't see the difference between science and fiction, so from time to time, we can trick the subconscious into feeling better. Smiling is just a trigger that immediately redirects your focus. The more you try it, the more natural and real it will feel, and the more helpful it will become.

You need a good night's sleep to have strong stress resistance. You need to relax to work productively. You need to feel good to enjoy your life and stay alert to the opportunities it brings. This all can be balanced and achieved by one simple action—smiling, and remembering that hearty laughter will allow you to get rid of all negativity that can easily get stored in you.

After a good, hearty laugh shared with friends, my cheeks hurt like I've been exercising, my entire body and mind are relaxed, and I feel calm and at ease. Even a few days later I just need to remember how we laughed together and the smile reappears on my face. It surely fills life with ease and beauty. We have the ability to laugh, and it's there for a good reason. In addition to dinners and serious events, plan fun times, games and activities that make you laugh with your friends and family, and you will all benefit from it.

• Smile to Support Your Immune System

As the levels of stress hormones are reduced when you smile, your immune system can get stronger. It can finally function properly without giving too much precious energy to fight stress. With a strong immune system, it's easier to survive cold winters and viruses, fight illnesses and simply stay healthy. Isn't that something we all truly need?

Smiling over time has proven to be helpful and a great support for healthy living. It's not a magic wand that makes anything happen. It's the force that comes through the smile. It's not the smile itself that shields your physical wellbeing. The smile is only the trigger. The force triggered by smiling is what does the magic to our bodies. It's a combination of physical and psychological influence that may change your life quality for the better.

When you laugh your body tissues receive more oxygen, blood flow increases and blood vessel functions are improved. Altogether, it is actually very good for your heart as well. Now laughter therapy (which is a real thing!) makes sense. If Joe the Baker laughed every single day just a little bit, he might support his immunity and heart. As an old Latin phrase says, "Mens sana in corpore sano," meaning that a healthy mind (or spirit) lives in a healthy body. Smiling is a natural act, and there is nothing negative about it. You may be surprised how much good smiling over time can do your body, and soul and there are zero side effects! Well, maybe only if you get infatuated with more smiles, but that's a good thing!

• Smile for Longer Life Expectancy

In regards to the idea that people with a positive outlook (for which a genuine smile is a clear sign) have happier lives, more stable personalities and relationships, psychologists Ernest Abel and Michael Kruger of Wayne State University held a study in 2010 in which they compared pictures of baseball players starting from 1952.[3] They analyzed the smiles of people in 230 pictures, taking into account other variables like education, career, marital status, year of birth and physical characteristics. When the study was conducted, most of the players had already died except those who had broad, genuine smiles. Even those players who smiled just a little bit in their pictures did better than those who didn't smile at all. The results of this study suggest that people who smile more have a life expectancy up to 5 to 7 years longer than people who don't smile.

People who smile more, are more satisfied with their lives

and more successful in what they do. We are used to thinking that successful people smile more than their unfortunate fellows simply because they are content because of their success—they don't have all those troubles unsuccessful people have. Of course they can smile! But science suggests that it's the other way round: if Joe the Baker started to smile more, he would become more successful as well. Your life doesn't become just more beautiful if you smile, but also helps you stay healthy. It's not a big surprise that healthy, happy people also can live longer because serious health issues simply don't affect them, and if they do become ill, it's simply easier to fight back with a positive mindset! While taking into account just one study that suggests smiling people might have longer life expectancy, we can't assume that everyone who smiles definitely lives longer. But there is something we can do: we can safely check it on ourselves because one thing is sure—if there are any side effects from smiling, they can only be positive and beneficial.

If you wait under the chandelier wondering why it's getting larger, it will most likely fall on you. Instead of just waiting you can take action, and the sooner you do it, the bigger the chances are that you will prolong your life!

• Smile for Support through Tough Times

Sometimes life goes uphill and sometimes it goes downhill, and when it goes downhill, it feels like we're falling terribly. Life can be hard either way, especially if we're facing troubles such as serious health issues, financial breakdowns or depressions. Sometimes all we want to do is to give up, but is that a solution? If you're already suffering, a negative mindset makes everything worse: one bad thing happens to you after another until your eyes and your mind gets blind to hope, new opportunities and positive changes. If you let the negativity take over your mind, you reject the possibility of positive outcomes and it becomes pretty easy to turn into wretch. That's not something I want to see in people around me.

With pure joy and appreciation, I look at people who sing, dance, laugh and enjoy what they have while having financial troubles or even fighting for their lives like those who are fighting cancer. The internet is full of inspiring videos of these people who stay happy contrary to popular expectations that they would break under the heaviness of their own troubles. They are the people who find solutions. They have the energy to fight. They are the ones who are inviting positive outcomes in their lives. Where do they get this energy from? From smiling. I'm thankful that the internet gives us the opportunity to find these inspiring stories. They help us zoom out and see our personal issues in a bigger picture. These inspiring stories aren't there just to kick us out of the comfort of sorrow and complaining, but they also prove that it's possible to choose another path to get through tough times. They prove the power of smile and positive mindset.

One smile leads to another, and that's how positivity grows in and around you. Don't make your hard times even worse by refusing positivity! By being grumpy, upset and feeding fears and hopelessness, you are just pushing yourself down. The lower you fall, the harder it becomes to get up and see the light again. Push a smile on your face when it hurts. Smile when it seems that everyone is expecting you to be unhappy. Smile when it feels like you are falling, and you will become unbeatable and unbreakable. I'm not saying that it's good to hide your real feelings and fake happiness all the time. Be authentic, let your negative feelings out, cry when you need to, but don't let the negativity become your normal state of mind. You need it from time to time and it might help you deal with some emotions. If all you have are depressive thoughts, fears, and sadness, however, anger will become part of your daily life, and you will be in serious danger. You become a desert—an abandoned place for draught and emptiness where flowers simply won't bloom. You drain all your energy trying to keep the desert moist and fruitful, but without any results. It even starts feeling that other people are turning away from you. They really turn away because each and every one of us is attracted to positivity and doesn't want someone else to bring them down by excess negativity. When everything goes down, the best you can do to get up again is work on a positive mindset. You can be a superhero in your own life by accepting smiling as your superpower! It's my superpower, and it can help you to get through hard times, too.

If you combine smiling with hearty laughter, it turns into a mild workout, providing more oxygen to your brain and body, burning calories and increasing productivity of your brain as well. It can definitely help you become stronger and feel better! Some physicians and exercising enthusiasts also say that smiling is like a full face workout that helps keep your face well-shaped and toned, even delaying skin sagging as we get older. It sounds pretty logical, although serious studies are still lacking in this field.

Taoist Master and teacher Mantak Chia (born on 1944) is probably the best teacher of what smiling means for your health. From Buddhist monks he learned meditation at the age of six, in his early years he was training in Thai Chi, Aikido and Yoga, and later started to study Taoist ideas and their approach to life. He learned from several famous, experienced spiritual teachers, mastered his ability to heal others, studied the Western approach to anatomy, gained deep, comprehensive knowledge about how the human body works and created the Universal Healing Tao system.

One of Taoist well-known teachings tells that all our inner organs and bodily systems are affected by emotional imbalances and negative emotions. He teaches Inner Smile practice to balance physical and mental health. All you have to do in this meditation is imagine abundant smiling energy, letting it inside of your body and directing it from one organ to another, filling them with smiling energy. There are five main points where the smiling energy enters: the heart, lungs, kidneys, liver and stomach. Directing smiling energy into each of these organs is beneficial in many ways: first, you acknowledge and feel these organs; second, you use the power of your own mind to clean and dissolve negativity in these organs; third, you fill them with positive energy. The smile doesn't even have to be in your face. All you need to smile for health is the inner smile. As the Master himself says, an inner smile is the root of inner alchemy. I encourage you to read more about Mantak Chia's inner smile practice and really learn it for yourself.

On a very basic level you can try to find your own feeling of inner smile right now. It won't be exactly what Mantak Chia means with the inner smile, because finding it requires some practice, but it will be a little something—the beginning of smiling for your health. Close your eyes and smile. Feel the pleasant feeling of smiling inside your body. Pay attention to how smiling changes your body and inner comfort levels. If you find that feeling inside yourself and repeat it regularly, you'll be able to recall it even without a physical smile on your face. Although your inner and physical smile come hand in hand, they can trigger each other. When you have found the feeling of your inner smile, direct this smiling energy to your heart. Just imagine it filling your heart, feel how this energy is enlightening your heart, filling and embracing your heart with joy and kindness. You can visualize this energy as light, you can simply feel it, and you can keep the smile on your face if it helps you to get the inner smile feeling. It can be a spiritual meditation, but it can also be mentally healing practice.

I truly suggest you work on finding your inner smile and let it spread through your body. We often poorly acknowledge who we are and what makes us who we are today. In hypnotherapy you can get an understanding of your inner self. You can also sort out problems your conscious mind has deleted, but subconsciously still keeps affecting your everyday life. With Mantak Chia's Inner Smile practice, you can put your mind and body in harmony; letting the inner smile into your body, you can learn how to feel your body better. It connects your awareness with the physical body in a beautiful, positive way. You can focus on your body parts and inner organs with heaviness or seriousness, but you can also do it through the lightness of smiling energy and let this positive energy dissolve the weight of different problems in your physical body.

Smiling people feel better and look better, and I do not care if they are young or old, defined as classical belles or unattractive beasts. Even the ugliest duckling will look much better and more attractive when smiling. So give me a reason why you don't want to be seen as a more appealing and better looking individual! If something is funny, don't suppress your smile and laughter! Let's take funny things seriously and let our smiles crack out for the sake of our own health and wellbeing! One thing is sure: there might be differences between us, but a genuine smile is more than just a positive facial expression. It's a medicine that's available to everyone. Smiling will make you happy, and happiness will make your life healthier and much more enjoyable.

5

The Magic of Mimicking

"Imitation is the sincerest form of flattery."
–Charles Caleb Colton, English cleric and writer

During an interesting conversation with an Irish girl, my friend suddenly realized he was copying her very distinct accent. He sounded like a comedian to himself, parodying the person he was talking to. Realizing this while in the middle of the conversation made him feel like he was mocking her, although that wasn't the case. He wasn't doing it intentionally. So, when he realized that he wasn't talking like he usually does, he started to worry about his speaking manner more than the conversation itself, and the discomfort began to grow. The conversation was interesting and pleasant, but he was surprised at himself for copying her speaking style and started to drift away in his thoughts: "Why am I doing it? Isn't it rude? I hope it doesn't offend her." She didn't even notice, but to him, it seemed like a pretty big deal.

What took place between these two people was a natural process called mirroring. In my friend's case, it happened unconsciously because of a pattern that already existed in his mind. When we sense and prove to ourselves over time that mirroring somebody else can make the other person feel more comfortable and more open to us, we establish a specific behavioral pattern that we can follow without even thinking about it. Like if you have learned that smiling can reduce stress, at the beginning you will consciously make yourself smile in stressful situations, but as time goes on, and smiling for you becomes a more and more familiar tool for stress reduction, you will do it without pushing yourself or even thinking about it.

The next time you see a mother feeding her baby, focus on her face. You will see her mouth open slightly and close as the baby eats. You will see how she mimics the baby's face while feeding it. I remember having always looked at my wife when she fed our baby. I was just not aware that I was doing exactly the same when I watched her! Mimicking and mirroring is a natural process, but it doesn't happen all the time. Consciously we all can imitate and mirror others while interacting, and when we focus on others and their actions, we imitate them without being aware of it. After a conversation with genuinely positive people, their smiles get into your face as well, even if you don't feel what they feel. You might soon feel that your cheeks start hurting from intensive smiling, but you can't help yourself. Smiles are contagious. Why do you sometimes respond to someone by mimicking their facial expressions? Why do we mimic expressions of others even if we don't have the same emotions? Is this just a dumb, unconscious action or is it there to help us in some strange way? How could mimicking someone else's smile help you?

Social psychologist Paula M. Niedenthal conducted a study to better understand the power of mimicking and why we need it.[4] For the experiment, she formed two groups of participants who had to observe changes in facial expressions of other people. One of the groups had to hold a pencil between their teeth while detecting changes in faces, and it limited their option to use their own facial expressions, so they couldn't imitate what they saw. The other group could use their own mimic freely, so when looking at pictures, they could imitate what they see. The group who could freely use their mimicking ability recognized emotions in other people better than those who couldn't use it. Turns out, it really is a special mechanism that helps us to identify emotional messages others are sending out.

The ability to mimic the expressions of others serves us in two ways:

1. We can detect and recognize the emotions of others when we mimic their expressions.

2. We can bond and make others feel more familiar and more comfortable if we have similar expressions and reactions.

It's called emotional cognition. We subconsciously mimic and imitate each other's emotional displays—from facial expressions to tone of voice, language use, posture and even movements. That's how we get information about other peoples' feelings. When we mirror them, we get deeper insight about what happens in other people. By mimicking a smile, you can actually figure out if it's a real or a fake one, and it can also help you to detect what emotions are making the person in front of you smile. It doesn't mean you have to mimic the expressions of others with the same intensity, but the mere ability to imitate what you see in others helps you understand what they're feeling.

You can also make someone else smile through them imitating your expressions. If your facial expression is negative, it's unpleasant to others, so do not expect them to reply with positivity. It won't come to them naturally. When you have a harsh, angry face, people will feel the need to protect themselves through fight or flight responses. People do not just mirror another's body language all the time, but if you send out happiness, they will be willing to receive and mirror it. A smile is something people will mirror. When you smile at them, they will smile back. If someone looks at you with a warm, kind smile, it will be brought into you as well. I bet you will be more attracted to the positive than the negative because it allows you to unlock your own positivity and feel the vibes that are related to satisfaction and pleasure.

There are special mirror-neurons in our brain that make us imitate one another to develop empathy. We mimic each other to make ourselves more familiar with others. It helps us fit in and feel more comfortable, to bond with other people and create personal relationships. It brings us closer and helps us understand each other's emotional processes better.

Our mirror-neurons are triggered by expressions of others, and with our facial expressions we trigger others to imitate us. Don't wait for someone else to be the first to smile! Be the first one who does it! If you approach the counter at a store, and the clerk smiles at you, you will smile back! If you were to approach the same counter and the person behind it was too busy with an old transaction to lift their head, but when they did, they found you smiling there, they would smile back! If you're BOTH looking at each other while you approach the clerk, and you smile first, he will most likely mirror you. You can be the one who comes to others with a smile and you will receive more smiles back than ever before. Mirroring exists and happens sometimes with our acknowledgement and sometimes without it. When it comes to smiling, dare to be the first one! Convince yourself that you can understand others better when you imitate them and you can also make them feel better and more comfortable with you if you share smiles with them!

The Game Changer in Your Face

Basically you can divide smiling into two major categories:

1. How you want OTHER people to perceive you at a given time.

2. How YOU feel or want to feel at a given time.

I'll focus first on how you feel, because when you feel good, you'll want to feel that way all the time, and then people will perceive you with the happiness and joy that you experience. They'll also subconsciously mimic you, and that's how you'll become associated with positive feelings in their minds. Remember that it's not just you who's mimicking others, but also others are mimicking you—purely subconsciously. Show an angry face, and most likely you won't get a friendly smile directed your way. Smile and you will receive a smile!

You're most likely to get new friends with a smile on your face. You're most likely going to get the best business deals if you carry a smile, and you can form positive, friendly relationships if you communicate with a smile on your face. You can also change the attitude of others and open them for communication with you. All you need is a smile.

A friendly smile, a confident smile or a flirtatious one—different smiles can help you in different situations. Sounds good, but I also understand that you simply might not know how to get, for example, that confident smile on your face for a job interview. Let's say you're highly skilled professional with experience and you're applying for a job that requires communication with other people. You have a stunning resume, and you're prepared for the interview. Of course, you're a little worried, so, you're doing your best to leave the impression of a serious, balanced person with the right attitude for the job. You know the right answers to tricky questions and you also look flawless. Everything will be fine.

When you arrive at the interview, you find out that it's going to be a group interview, so you'll be able to see the other people applying for the same opening. Everyone in the group seems pretty well prepared, suitable for the opening, and has the main professional skills needed for the job. Joe, who answers questions right after you, doesn't have as much experience as you. He doesn't have that much to say about how professional he is, so, he chooses to talk about his personality and does so with a smile. He takes time to answer questions and his answers sometimes seem a bit odd. He sometimes even seems to understand that his answers aren't perfect and when it happens, he smiles. You notice that the interviewer smiles back. Actually, you all do, and not because he has said something funny, but because he seems like a nice, friendly man. However, as the interview goes on, you discover that you really have the most relevant experiences and the most correct answers. It seems to you that the interview went well. So, now you just have to wait for the answer.

A few days later you get the answer—they have chosen another candidate. You saw them all, so why not you? Then who got the job? Maybe Sally who had similar work experience as you? Or maybe Peter who seemed very well prepared for the interview? Arrogant Claire? Shy Suzie? Or that young girl who seemed so afraid to talk that you didn't even hear her name properly? No, it was Joe—the one who seemed to be far from perfect, but had a smile in his face. When he smiled, he caused others to mimic him, and that's how he made a positive impression. Even if everyone in the room understood that he wasn't the most qualified, he was emotionally attractive because of his smile. Without proper skills and experiences he might not be the fit for technical position, but for working at a customer service he definitely wins.

If you ever have to compete for a date or the best price

at the flea market with smiling Joe, he'll always have a better chance than any other grounded, well-prepared person in the room. If I had to choose a person to hire for an interpersonal job, or to arrange my schedule and meetings with others, I would go to smiling Joe. Why? Because you can teach him, he can learn, practice and develop his professional skills just like everyone else, but unlike other people, it'll be easier and more pleasurable to work with a person who has a positive, friendly attitude that will eventually reflect positively on me and my company. I mean, there is nothing wrong with being well-prepared, serious and highly professional, and when it comes to jobs, smiling alone often can't do the job. Just remember that a smile can increase your chances and opportunities. It's a powerful tool that changes not just your inner world, but also the way others perceive you.

Mimic What's Missing in Your Life

When you subconsciously mimic the smile of another person you're also letting in the feelings that stand behind a smile of that other person. You connect and get closer to them. It doesn't always happen consciously, but that doesn't mean you're powerless in front of your own human nature. You can develop your ability to smile in different situations if you consciously play with mimicking smiles. Intentionally mimicking a specific type of a smile is kind of like faking a smile—you're trying to communicate not the feelings that are already in you, but the feelings that you trigger by smiling.

Let's work with the same confident smile we already mentioned. We would all love to arrive for job interviews like the confidently smiling people from business ads, but for most of us, inner feelings of fear, doubt and lack of confidence simply do not allow us to do it. If you have trouble communicating confident smiling when dealing with someone who is in a higher position than you (your boss, a person you appreciate, an interviewer etc.), try to mimic smiles of confident business people.

1. Observe

First, observe them—what makes them to look so confident? How are they smiling? Is that the same smile a person would have meeting his best friend or is it slightly different? What makes their smile attractive? Why do they look confident smiling this specific way? Check pictures and videos of confidently smiling people and try to identify what makes them to appear confident. Are their postures and gestures adding to that smile?

2. Mimic

The best way to understand how they do it is to mimic their smile just like trying on new clothes at the store. Mimic the smile of a confident person. Naturally the first feeling is that it triggers a specific kind of facial expression through which those inner feelings project. When you mimic a facial expression you can also catch the feeling that is standing behind similar expressions. When you've done your work observing, try that smile on! Just look at the picture or video of a specific smiling person you consider confident and try to mimic their smile.

3. See yourself

Step in front of the mirror with the same facial expression and try to perfect it to match the smile you are trying to mimic.

4. Feel it

Let in the feelings the confident smile brings! How do you feel looking into the mirror and seeing yourself confidently smiling? Do you feel strong and charming? If not, imagine the results you want this smile to bring. Imagine the success and confidence it gives, and feel it. You can also close your eyes to enjoy imaginative pictures and let positive feelings of confidence spread throughout your body. Tell yourself, "I am strong. I am confident. I am positive. I know my worth." Then open your eyes and see yourself in the mirror again. When the feeling is within you, it projects on your face. When you put some effort into feeling what you want to feel, the feeling becomes real.

5. Reinforce

Repeat it: observe, mimic, see yourself, feel it and see yourself once again. It's an exercise that will help your conscious mind accept this feeling as natural. By reinforcement, you can make this confident smile a part of yourself, and it soon won't be fake anymore. It will become real, and it doesn't matter if your mind isn't bright, your skills aren't well developed and you still have a long way to go; reinforcing the confident smile will open the gate and bring you closer to what you want.

An old Latin proverb says, "Fortune favors the bold." We are more than 2,000 years away from the times when this saying appeared, and I will be daring enough to say that times have changed. Fortune favors those who smile. Smiling is a powerful tool in the world where your success often depends on how others perceive you. The paradox is that you are the one who creates the link between yourself and others. You are the one who makes others perceive you in a specific way. Try on this smile every day, give it your attention and you will unlock its natural way to your face and to hearts of others.

6. Experiment with mimicking

You can experiment with mimicking different smiles, not just a confident one. Try an attractive smile, a shy smile, a flirtatious smile, a comforting smile or a mysterious smile. Observe the smiles you like and are attracted to, and mimic them to understand what feelings lie behind them. Use the same exercise with different smiles: observe, mimic, see yourself, feel it and see yourself once again. If you know how it should feel, soon it will be easy for you to bring out the right feeling for a smile when it's needed. Play in your head different situations in which the smile you are trying to mimic would be appropriate and desirable. Imagine yourself in those situations while physically mimicking the desirable smile. Repeat it again and again, and it will get stored in your memory as the right thing to do when you get in those situations.

Then take it to the next level: mimic smiles that you have tried at home in specific situations, and then check how they work on other people. Check if the smiles you've learned are changing the facial expressions of others. If the smile you mimic according to imaginative pictures in your head leaves others indifferent, practice more! When the smile you once learned to mimic becomes a natural for you, the magic happens.

Also, don't forget that you can make yourself more appealing to others by mimicking their smiles. When you talk to a smiling person, imitate what you see and you'll get more familiar with and closer to them, which leads to positive associations when they think about you.

Looking at the Grumpy Cat pictures is fun only online. Nobody actually wants to communicate with someone who has a Grumpy Cat aura and facial expressions in real life. The ability to mimic and imitate is a great power we all have. So use it! Play with it, experiment with it, and it will make your life easier. It might feel fake in the beginning, but that's something you can solve with time and practice.

6

Real and Fake Smiles

"Wear a smile and have friends; wear a scowl and have wrinkles."
George Eliot, English novelist, journalist, translator

All those smiles aren't the same, right? Mona Lisa's charming smirk isn't really the same as a smile that forms on your face when you are positively surprised. And the smile you get from your date after telling a joke isn't the same smile you carry during vacation or the one that warms your heart when bringing good news to someone. Smiles come from satisfaction, joy and happiness. Sometimes feelings of dominance and comfort, surprise, bravery, gratitude, fun or confidence can bring out smiles as well, but sometimes we smile without those positive feelings. Sometimes we even fake our smiles.

Here is a list of reasons we fake smiles:

- to be polite
- to fit in
- to make others trust us
- to hide our real emotions
- to create a positive impression
- to show support and acceptance
- to encourage someone else to smile
- because we are expected to smile in specific situations

We fake smiles not just when we consciously acknowledge we're supposed to smile. It doesn't matter if your logical, analytic mind knows how beneficial smiling is to you. Your intuitive, subconscious mind doesn't need theoretical knowledge and written proof because it already knows that smiling brings changes, and from time to time, the subconscious mind forces you to fake a smile. Sometimes it happens when you're talking to a person you don't like, when you hear a stupid joke and other times in place of a harsh response to someone's stupid claims. Instead of getting angry, you just put on a fake smile. No words at all, just one small fake smile that looks the same as a real one, yet feels different.

Can we hide our true feelings in fake smiles, projecting our message without letting others know how we truly think and feel? Politicians, businessmen, models, actors, different public figures have learned to use this skill. From time to time, we all do it in social situations. We'll smile even if we don't feel like it. I know that "fake" doesn't sound nice if genuineness is one of your values. I truly appreciate genuineness and authenticity, but it doesn't mean you should never fake a smile. Even fake smiling comes with some benefits, but first we need to learn how to recognize fake and real smiles.

The Difference to See

Subconsciously we read the emotional information behind smiles when interacting with someone else. We see the surroundings, we hear the language a person is using, the manner of speaking, we see their eyes, body language and sense their attitudes. Reading this information depends also on our relationships—on how well we know each other, how much time we've spent together and how open we are each to other. The better you know a person, the better you can read his or her facial expressions. Most want to read facial expressions in order to know someone better. It makes them to feel like wizards. Knowing what happens in other person's mind is truly an empowering feeling. On the other hand, if all your colleagues at work tomorrow suddenly could read your mind, you might get slapped every hour. Or maybe they would hug you?

Everyone can learn to distinguish between real and fake smiles and I believe that everyone should try, because it really helps better understand other people and improves communication and relationships.

One of us reads facial expressions better; another isn't that good at it. If you don't see yourself as someone who can recognize body language, know that it's like everything in life: it's a learning process. You might have that ability in you, but haven't yet opened up to take a good look and recognize it.

Some people are great at observations, others just use intuition. Knowledge and experience will lead you to better intuitive recognition, and you can train it. It takes just some knowledge, attention, observing, focusing and being open minded. These traits can make you an expert in recognizing what stands behind smiles. I can recognize when people are smiling genuinely and when they are faking, and you can do it too. If you aren't gifted with strong intuitive recognition skills (or most likely, you just haven't discovered or developed those skills), there are also clearly visible signs of real and fake smiles.

Remember what you've read previously: a genuine smile is like a full-face exercise and it involves your entire face, not just the muscles around your mouth. Genuine smiling is not just a wide open mouth showing your teeth. That can be a fake smile as well, just like a shy, barely visible smile can come from real emotions. Real and fake smiles can be very similar, although it's possible to recognize the difference.

Lips

Lips are the main things to pay attention to when you spot a smile. When observing smiles, we primarily pay attention to the lips and how they are contracted. There aren't smile lines that are always fake or always genuine. For one person, a broad smile that reveals teeth is a natural way to smile while others express their joy and happy feelings with barely visible smiles. What says the most is the intensity of the smile.

A smile with a closed mouth, tight lips and low intensity shows unspoken and implicit emotions behind the visible picture—something isn't real there, something that a person is hiding, yet willing to appear friendly. Polite and correct—it's there, it's present, polite, friendly and better than no smile at all. For example, these smiles are often seen at job interviews—people who are interviewed want to leave a good impression, yet they aren't confident enough, don't fully understand the information they receive or don't want to reveal too much about themselves. It's also a sign of stress and nervousness. That's how you look when experiencing discomfort, yet willing to appear friendly or show that you understand the information being given to you.

The same closed mouth smile with tight lips, but high intensity (and maybe even some teeth revealed) truly shows friendliness and openness. However, it doesn't say, "I'm fully open to you!" It still draws a line of privacy between people, which is only natural when meeting them for the first time. Of course, you don't start sharing private details about your family life with strangers, or your passwords and intimate feelings. You're also not going to hug them like you hug good friends, but if you're opened to this new communication, this is the smile that shows it—a genuine smile of friendliness and openness, and without secret meanings. This smile appears on our faces when we are relaxed and willing to have friendly communication.

When you spot a closed-mouth smile, pay attention to the body language as well. At times closed body language (like, crossed arms and legs) resembles discomfort or unwillingness to share something. The same as with a closed mouth smile that it might indicate a personal feeling, but might also happen because a person has, for example, undesirable looking teeth. It simply makes them less open to you as you'd like.

When just one side of the mouth is pulled up, forming a half-smile, it might indicate a sarcastic attitude or conflicting emotions. You can see it directed to you when someone doubts your ideas and considers his are better. It slips onto faces of people who are pretending that they're listening while actually elsewhere in their thoughts. It decorates faces of confused people and those who are considering conflicting thoughts. A half-smile can appear on a face of an arrogant person who smiles out of politeness; it can stand for half-love, half-genuineness or a half of any other feeling expressed through the smile.

A smirk or a sneer—a mocking, arrogant, irritatingly smug smile—shows the feeling of dominance, superiority over you and self-satisfaction. A smirk can also appear on the face of a person who is being verbally attacked, and in that case it can show disbelief to what is told and confusion. Finally, the broad smile revealing teeth is the most honest and sincere one, although it's possible to fake that one as well.

If there are 5 pictures with different smiling faces in them, and you cover those faces to see just mouths, it's actually pretty hard to read the emotions behind those smiles. How do you know if that half-smile is formed by confusion or sarcastic attitude? How do you know if that broad smile comes from genuine joy or is it there because it is used as a professional tool to convince you? The term "Pan American Smile"—a broad smile that doesn't involve eyes and muscles around the eyes—describes smiling in a polite manner. This is the professional tool that might help you in many cases, yet it's also a smile without genuine feelings behind it. It's formed only by the lips, without involving other parts of the face, and sometimes it might look fake and feel cold. A genuine smile isn't formed only by lips, so, you have to pay attention to other signs as well.

Eyes

The mouth resembles what the eyes see, but the eyes in most cases cannot lie. It's no wonder that eyes are called the mirror of our souls. They allow us to see the world, but they also tell other about our inner worlds, which include our feelings and thoughts. Only professional actors who know how to fully get into character know how to express themselves totally and completely. You might agree that many times you'll see an actor in action and you'll say, "Wow, he's a great actor!" Why? Because you felt that he was fully in that moment. Most people are not professional actors, and life is not a movie or a play.

When identifying what stands behind smiles, check if there's eye contact. A person who avoids eye contact isn't fully open and might be hiding something or feel uncomfortable. Eye contact makes communication personal, and if you're not willing to open up, it's just easier to look away or at some feature of a person's face besides directly into their eyes. Lying is hard while looking into the eyes of a person you know you are lying to, the same as it's hard to hide something from a person you maintain eye contact with.

But eye contact really does magic if you're willing to create friendly relationships and honest communication. (Of course, you can go to extremes with obtrusive staring, which might be pretty creepy. So please avoid doing this.) The one who unnaturally and insistently stares at you with eyes wide open wishes to take control over you or to convince you of something. People who are close can naturally keep eye contact for longer, but even they don't stare at each other insistently. Wide open eyes and a hearty smile don't go together because facial muscles just don't work that way. Wide open eyes while smiling is a clear sign of expressing fake emotions. That's what you often see in the faces of people posing for pictures.

A genuine positive smile takes over the face. It narrows eyes and displays little wrinkles around the eyes also called laugh lines or crow's feet. These tiny wrinkles at the outer corners of the eyes that have got their name because of the resemblance with a footprint of a crow. A genuine feeling behind a smile can change the position of eyebrows and tighten forehead. When genuineness is expressed, nobody thinks of how that smile looks—it always looks good because it comes with positive energy and real emotions, and no matter how wide or intensive the smile is, it involves the entire face.

Try to compare pictures of celebrities. In professional photo shoots, their broad smiles are often accompanied with wide open eyes and not the smallest wrinkle. Of course, today Photoshop comes in the game as well, helping us get rid of beautiful smile wrinkles, but check older pictures of, for example, charming Marilyn Monroe. You'll notice that her broad smile in professional photo shoots is different than in pictures from her personal collection and private moments. The difference is not in lips or revealed teeth, but in the eyes!

Can you laugh without smile wrinkles in your face? Honest laughter just like a broad, natural smile doesn't come without those smile wrinkles. I just tried it in front of a mirror to get proof. Try it, and you'll also see.

One more thing to remember: a person who doesn't avoid eye contact and doesn't try to keep it for too long while smiling communicates real emotions.

Body Language

Body language is a big field to study and nothing here is carved into stone. People have the desire to organize information about ourselves and announce a few observations as general rules. The truth is that logic and science in this field don't give answers that are universal or allow us to read other people the same way in all situations and circumstances. We feel, we perceive and understand many things subconsciously, but are these rules? Not always. You have to keep an open mind and use your intuition.

It doesn't matter how deep your knowledge of body language is, you can always pay attention to it and get more insights into people around you by simple observations. Body language of a smiling person can give you clearer answers of what is happening behind the smile. Stiffness might show feelings of discomfort, while open gestures like uncrossed arms and legs could show openness. On the other hand, crossed arms don't always mean that a person is not willing to open up. It might simply be that it is cold, and some gestures and postures depend on the comfort of clothes a person is wearing. Someone trying to tell lies will avoid eye contact and keep arms crossed, while an experienced liar could confidently lie to you while also looking absolutely comfortable and relaxed. You have to learn how to see the entire picture.

From your first day on Earth, you learn body language. We all use body language to reflect our intentions, not emotions.

You might not feel confident, but you force yourself to push back your shoulders, straighten your spine and rise your chin when you want to look and feel more confident. Plus, we will add a suitable facial expression—sometimes trying to hide what we feel, but sometimes in order to make others discern us the way we want them to see us. We won't get too deep into discussing body language in this book, since our focus is mainly on facial expressions. We read most of the emotional information from faces of others, but seeing the entire picture might really bring a change in understanding others better and improving communication and relationships with them. Just pay attention to the body language of others and feel it, even if you don't fully understand it. Then you'll be also able to make yourself better understood.

To learn reading body language better, you can also try different postures on yourself. Like in a theatre class, try to imagine and copy, and then reflect on what you feel and how it looks on you! How a relaxed person sits and stands? How confident people move? What gestures shy people use and what posture do they take while sitting? What does a bored person look like? When you're trying to copy gestures and postures of people in different situations, your body learns and your computer—the mind—gains new knowledge. You can learn a lot from yourself as well! From the previous chapter you already know that we all unconsciously use mimicking to affect interpersonal interaction, and it works, helping us understand others better and also to adjust our own emotional displays to the expressions of other people.

Micro-expressions

Although you can fake your facial expressions, there is something researchers call micro-expressions. No matter what you are trying to show or prove, the truth at some point will appear on your face—it might be just for a short moment, a second or even less, that reveals the real emotion. You can keep your wide smile signaling friendliness, but if you are trying to hide with this smile arrogance, at some point for a very short moment your smile will turn into a cold smirk, which then disappears. With some training and development of your observation skills, you can learn to spot micro-expressions in faces of others. Focus, observe and reflect— it will take you far!

The fact that science can't give you the perfect dictionary of body language and guide to reading facial expressions yet doesn't mean that you can't use it to improve interaction with other people. You already do it every day. As I mentioned previously, we simply feel many things, often even more than we can understand. The brain puts together information from many different shelves in our personal libraries, and we get the feeling, sometimes unexplainable and irrational, but still—it's there and it has some kind of reason. Sometimes you need to just trust your first impression. What comes to your mind first in many cases is your first impression, which comes directly from your gut feeling. Any impression after this will be translated by your conscious mind, and at time altered with doubt and conflicts. Trust your first impression.

To Fake or Not To Fake?

Of course, if you truly are friendly, opened and positive-minded, you don't need to fake your smile—it's just there, simply and naturally, but keeping yourself positive-minded and opened can be difficult at the end of exhausting day. You're the same friendly person, but if it feels like you've spent all your positive energy and the only thing you want is just some rest and peace, faking a broad smile might feel like additional work. So can faking a smile be beneficial or is it just a purely bad thing to do?

In 2011, Brent Scott of Michigan State University conducted a study to discover the difference between the results of forced and authentic smiling.[5] For two weeks researchers followed a group of people who have to interact with dozens of people daily so they are more subjected to fake smiling. The study discovered that in days when people had to suppress their negative emotions and force smiling, they felt withdrawn, while on days when they felt positive, cultivated positive mindset and effortlessly shared real emotion based smiles, not just their mood, but also their productivity was boosted.

One forced smile won't make a big difference, but if you have to force yourself for the entire day—for example, if you work a customer service job—then most likely you won't come home satisfied. It means that forced smiling can make your bad day even worse. So, how to survive those bad days with a smile in your face? The answer is by cultivating a positive mindset. But don't throw out the idea of faking smiles! To fake it or not? If asked this question, I would say: "Fake it till you make it!"

Authentic smiling brings more benefits than fake smiling, but, yes, I am advising you here to fake smiling. It might take more of your mental energy than authentic smiling, but it's not a useless action. I do believe that if a smile at the beginning doesn't come naturally, you can fake it to push yourself to smile more. The moment you fake a smile, you do have a happy face and the natural mechanism starts making you feel better. Of course, you will be happier if the smile comes from the heart, but the subconscious mind takes what you are giving. If you use repetition, at some point the conscious mind will open its critical factor – the gate that separates the critical mind from our subconscious mind. The subconscious mind will then start accepting your action as real. Your intentional fake smiling will turn into natural smiling.

Just like forming any new habit, for a few days, it's not easy because your mind is used to something different, but as you put efforts into committing to your new activity, it becomes your reality. For example, if you want to make a 15 minute long meditation a part of your morning routine, it might be hard to concentrate or even find time for it at the beginning, but as you push through the first days, your mind gets used to it. If you put efforts in doing it every morning for 3 weeks, in the 4th you'll wake up ready for meditation and never skip it again because it will simply turn into a natural process like having breakfast.

I'm not asking you to walk around with a fake smile on your face all the time, but in some situations or while working on cultivating positivity and changing your mindset, fake it! Remember that even if your smile isn't coming from the heart, it makes you look younger, more beautiful, approachable and friendly. Not just a genuine smile, but also the conscious effort you put into getting a smile on your face improves your communication with others and opens doors!

Basically, if fake smiling were useless, at least half of smiles around the world would disappear. So, is fake smiling really a bad thing? Not always! Sometimes people share a fake smile with you not because they intend to hide something from you, but because they have the best intentions to show you their friendliness even if they feel tired or melancholic. Your own fake smile isn't always on your face to mislead people. If you haven't yet developed a truly positive mindset, your good intentions matter more that if your smile is real or fake. Sometimes all we need or all we can give is a comforting smile, and it's great that there's someone to give it to us or someone to whom we can offer our smiles. In those situations real or fake doesn't matter. What matters is the goodwill behind a smile.

I would suggest having a small smile each time you walk around in public, and even when you're alone in your house. Get yourself used to having a little smile on. Even if your mouth doesn't move, let your eyes feel happiness – happiness for the beautiful day, happiness for the life you have, happiness for the health and happiness for just being here for another day. When your eyes feel this happiness the face will project it in a very small yet un-ignorable smile that will make you feel good about yourself and others around you!

Faking a smile might feel wrong sometimes, but keep going—fake it till you make it! Reinforcement is what forms new habits and new patterns in your mind. Repetition is what reinforces changes in you, so, make sure you reinforce the right things, allowing them to change your life!

7

It All Starts with You

*If you're not using your smile, you're like a person with a
million dollars in the bank and no checkbook!"*
– Les Giblin, Self-help author

I believe that by reading this book, you have already gotten
many ideas about how such a simple thing like your own
smile can change your life. It affects your mood, your
wellbeing, health and success, your communication and
relationships with others. If you come with a smile in order to
make a difference in your surroundings, you can overcome
unpleasant obstacles easier, build closer relationships and
unlock your potential to change the reality you live in. In the
following chapters, we'll discuss what specific changes you
can initiate and encourage with your smile.

The emotional information that comes with and through

our smiles is beyond calculation or measure, but without it, a smile by purely physical measures is still a smile, and that's what many enthusiastic researchers have tried to understand by bringing us proof that smiling truly is beneficial. You knew it anyways, right? You feel the power of smiling the same way as I do. The mind truly is a mysterious place. There are many things we clearly feel and observe, but we have a tendency to doubt and question before we allow ourselves to believe. You have to question everything around you because your mind needs something to process. You have to look for proof to accept new ideas and perspectives available to you, but if you allow your mind to deny every situation, idea and any kind of new information, you're cutting off many options that might work for you. You know that a smile holds positive and immense power. If you're skeptical, now is a good time to make a change and open your mind to other possibilities. Being skeptic is okay; you don't need to be gullible. However, you shouldn't block things either. Keep an open mind, experiment, check what smiling does to you and your life, and your mind will explore new possibilities.

You know that a smile is more than just contracted muscles. It's also more than just an expression of happiness. A smile has value on your physical, emotional and mental levels. It can heal you on all those levels, and also on the interpersonal level. To find out how smiling can affect and change different fields of your life, let's start with the closest thing you have—your inner world. Besides creating positive impressions and looking happier, smiling provokes changes inside of you. Actually, it all starts within you: a trigger for a smile, positive emotion, a response to someone else's smile.

A smile starts from you just like love, peace and positivity, and many other essential things that form our lives don't come from outer space, but are born within us.

• Smile to Keep Calm & Do the Best You Can

Any research assumes that something is undiscovered, denied, poorly understood or existent even if denied. It always assumes that our knowledge is not yet complete. To investigate the power of smiles, many studies around the world have used chopsticks. When you place a chopstick or a pencil in your mouth and hold it with your teeth without your lips touching it, it involves the same muscles that form real smiles, but without the emotional information accompanying smiles. Of the numerous studies and experiments conducted to discover the power of a smile, the following one is of particular interest:

We know that positivity lowers our stress levels—we feel it and science supports this idea, but in 2012 Tara L. Kraft and Sarah D. Pressman of University of Kansas conducted a study to understand if manipulating positive facial expressions would positively affect our responses to stress.[6] Basically, would putting a fake smile on when you don't feel like smiling help us do better in stressful situations? 170 participants who didn't know the purpose of the experiment were asked to do stressful tasks holding chopsticks in their mouths in 3 different manners that physically look like expressions of real emotions: 1) in a way that creates a wide smile (called also Duchenne smile), 2) just a normal, casual smile, 3) and a neutral facial expression. So, there were two smiling groups and one neutral. Half the participants in smiling groups were directly asked to smile consciously while completing tasks, but others didn't receive any instructions. What the experiment revealed was that all of the smiling participants (not just those who were asked to smile, but also the people who had smiling expressions due to holding chopsticks in their mouths) had lower heart rates after completing the tasks when recovering from stressful situations than those who had no smile in their faces at all. This experiment showed that smiling (whether fake and unconscious or intentional and genuine) has a positive effect on stress reduction on both physical and psychological levels. The researchers also noticed that the participants with the big (Duchenne) smiles on their faces had a slight advantage in keeping the heart rates lower.

We simply do better with smiles on our faces! Positive facial expressions supply us with physiological and psychological benefits, even if we are not aware of the act of smiling. When you smile and your brain releases those feel good chemicals, they quickly lower your cortisol (stress hormone) levels, and a calm heart helps keep the mind calm as well.

So many modern health issues are caused by increased stress levels. It drives us to depression, mental and physical disorders, and is a serious threat to our lives. Stress kills people every day. Seed in your head the thought that smiling is helpful and get used to having a smile on your face every day because we have to recognize stress and prevent it. I'm just like you: a person who isn't fully free from rising stress levels. From time to time when something goes wrong or something unexpected happens, I too experience stress, but when I hear that stress knocking on the door, I don't let it in. Instead, I take a deep breath and find my smile. It doesn't have to be a big, shiny smile. Even a little smile or just your inner feeling of smiling can push the stress out.

Use smiles as a preventing method for any stress related matters. When a situation arises, use it as a leverage to swing the negative into the positive. That reminds me that as a very fat child, I learned Judo sport. I was very fat and not that fast, however, I chose Judo because it uses your enemy's force to your advantage. In Judo, you take your enemy and use his weight or speed against him in order to make him fall. Then you can pin him down. Use smiling in the same way. Take advantage of negativity to remind yourself how much of good there is out there—anything to bring your smile on your face and positive feelings in your heart. Sometimes we need to have a bit of salt to remind ourselves how sweet sugar is!

If you can't deal with yourself to the degree that you can't even push yourself to smile, keep a chopstick in your pocket! It will indeed look funny to everyone else when you put a chopstick in your mouth, forcing your muscles to contract in a smile-like formation. Just imagine: you are arrive at a hotel and the receptionist greets you holding a chopstick in her teeth. You can do it too! Of course, you can also learn to deal with your stress and put a smile on your face.

• Smile to Change Your Mood & Get Things Done

Stress management becomes much easier if you have a positive mindset. Getting through conflict situations, moving towards your goals and overcoming difficulties is easier if you have positive mindset—a set of positive attitudes that defines your behavior. You might not be the most optimistic person in the world, but you can learn to maintain a positive mindset, seeing the bright side of small troubles and looking for beauty and pleasure. At the end of the day, who is the biggest beneficiary of your smile? Your boss, your spouse and anyone else that comes in your way might benefit, but the biggest winner here is you.

Many people allow their own negative emotions to trap them in bad moods. They even get angry at themselves for not being in a good mood. Like getting mad about being in a bad mood could make things better! When teens come home from school with sad faces because they have homework to do, they are only seeing the negative side of things. I think homework is fantastic: you get to do it on your own time, at home and without the pressure of the teacher or others who do it faster or slower than you. Here is the chance to check yourself for perfection! If fact, there is more good than bad!

Remember the brain chemistry we discussed previously! When you smile, your brain is producing "feel good chemicals" simply making you feel better and find positivity, no matter what tasks or duties you have to complete. What's the magic wand to change your mood from bad to good? Your smile!

You are not trapped in your own emotions and you are not limited by the options you have here and now. You have a powerful computer (your mind) and a great tool (your body) to make the best out of every day of your life. With the help of a smile, you can change your brain chemistry and make yourself feel good. And it doesn't cost a thing! Contracting your face in the expression of smiling is like pressing your "smile button," which starts the machine sending signals to the brain in loops that activate your brain chemistry.

When your dishwasher is broken and a pile of dirty dishes is filling your kitchen sink, it might be hard to get up and finally do the job, especially after a big dinner with your family. You feel lazy, you procrastinate, you are trying to find someone else to do it, but nothing changes—dirty dishes aren't going to wash themselves. You might even start to look for reasons not to do it, maybe you feel sleepy, or maybe your legs are tired. You can keep finding an endless ocean of excuses, but the dishes will still be there. If you have to do something you simply don't want to, don't wait until there are ten more new tasks. Get up, put a smile on your face, and find joy in unpleasant tasks! Many things simply seem big and bad, boring, dirty and unpleasant just because you think about them negatively. Put a smile on your face when you feel lazy, upset, nervous, anxious or sad, and let the magic happen!

You don't always have to be in good mood. We all have our own ups and downs. So be honest with yourself, but write it in your mind: a bad mood is no longer an excuse. Now you know how to alleviate it at least a little bit!

• Smile for Confidence

I don't know any situation in which healthy self-confidence can't help. It doesn't matter from which angle you look at it. It's necessary for success. You can be an actor, retailer, entertainer, student, nurse, teacher, fireman or anyone else—self-confidence isn't just a savior in many situations, but it also allows you to acknowledge and enjoy yourself. A self-confident person isn't the one who glorifies and praises himself, but knows his or her worth. A self-confident person isn't the one who sticks his nose in the clouds, but also not the one who denies himself. You might make mistakes, you might have less than you want to have, you might not know how to get yourself out of life's troubles, and despite of your efforts, the neighbor's yard will still look greener. If you are a self-confident person, however, finding the way out always is a lot easier.

You might think that you don't have this and that, but when you think of all the things that you *do* have, you will realize that many people in the world can only dream of having this lifestyle. Life is all about how you see the world and yourself in it. You can always find a million of things that you lack, yet also two million things and reasons that make you prosperous and fortunate. If you see what you already have, it can make you happy. When you see the good things, you allow your life to be fulfilled with happiness and joy. Remind yourself everyday how fortunate you are, and this will give you two million reasons to smile!

The one who lacks self-confidence will simply stay in one spot grieving and becoming more fearful, while a self-confident person will step out to reach another place, get help or find the street signs that lead to the desired place. Confident people are the ones who are the bosses of their own lives. They go into the world with a smile, and it seems that they're the ones who take it all—money, friendships, great relationships, the best jobs and even a better sandwich than their colleagues. Just a smile isn't enough to build a healthy self-confidence that will help you move through the life and get the most out of it, but it's a big, underrated and truly helpful tool that can boost your confidence.

Smiling isn't necessary just for sharing with others. It also plays a significant role for your inner self. Smiling is like welcoming what you truly want to come into your life.

Take a deep breath, smile and imagine your smile taking you over and warming or cooling you down (whichever seems more suitable for each situation) when:

- you want to feel safe and secure
- you need energy and confidence to move on
- you are looking for a solution
- you are on the way to important meeting
- you are looking for support
- you want to feel connected with others
- you are looking for the right direction in your life
- you want to feel strong and capable of following your heart
- you seek inner peace and harmony within yourself
- and when you need a reminder of those 2 million reasons that make your life wonderful, abundant and fulfilled.

Put a smile on your face and focus on your smile to let it spread through your mind. Your mind will accept it and let it work for you!

Just one more thing to remember: it's not the wide smile that's necessary for enjoying the benefits of smiling, but keeping positivity in your face. A smiling face comes from your heart and that's what makes the difference – a happy face that's like a calm gesture, an invitation that shows interest, enjoyment, willingness to share and even more. Try to find in yourself that spark of positivity and keep it in your eyes! If you feel your inner smile, it will reflect on your face even if it's just a barely visible smile, not a broad one. If your eyes are smiling your smile is genuine, even if nobody can spot it in your face as contracted lips to form a smile-line.

After high school when I was 18, I went on a one-month long backpacking trip with my best friend from school: Ohad. We went all the way from Italy to London and stopped to explore every country. One of the most memorable places for me was Switzerland, where we took a trip to one of the tallest mountains in the country. Getting there required a slow 3–4 hour train ride. The landscape behind the window was truly magnificent, but even more impressive was the man sitting facing us. He was a seemingly ordinary man who stuck in my head and still makes me to smile many years later. He was probably in his seventies, if not more, wearing a typical Swiss pants with suspenders and a multicolored shirt. His head was nearly bald, and he had extremely red cheeks. He didn't speak a word of English, so I wasn't able to have a conversation with him. He was looking through the window, holding a nylon bag with pieces of yellow cheese and a small knife in his hand. While the train was slowly moving higher up the mountains, the man in front of us was cutting small pieces of cheese, eating it, watching the landscape and smiling the whole trip. Ohad and I were amazed from the positive energy of that old man. He didn't seem rich at all. He was old and physically limited, but he was so happy enjoying every scene on the way and every bite of his cheese. His smiling face, small blue, shiny eyes and red cheeks are engraved in my memory to this very day. He was radiating positivity, satisfaction and happiness. He didn't need much, just smiling towards life. This man has changed my life. I remember and see him every day when I feel down. He is my trigger and anchor to the beauty of life, always reminding me that it's all about the way you see life through your eyes and how you process it in your mind.

8

Smile for Your Professional Success

"If at first you don't succeed... so much for skydiving."
-Henny Youngman, American comedian and violinist

When you feel good, your self-confidence grows. How much more could you do in your life if you had more confidence? A lot more! Lack of confidence is the biggest obstacle that holds us back from reaching our dreams, climbing up the career ladder, approaching people and building new relationships. Of course, this lack of confidence is often backed by fear, doubt and negative emotions. You have a perfect and easy-to-use method that can change it—smile, do it regularly and do it more! People in professional situations smile to create a positive image and trust, but even more, they do it to appear skillful and confident. It works, because it really makes them self-confident.

Do you think public speakers always smile just because they're happy with their lives? Many of them are nervous before public performances, even after they've done it for years, but a smile can save the situation! It will block negativity, help relieve stress, make you feel better, and if everything else falls apart, at least you've created the image of a positive person. That's a lot, because it'll attract people to you.

• Smile to Create The First Impression that Counts

The first impression you get when you meet someone defines your future communication and your possible relationship. If there's a grumpy face on you, it's most likely that you aren't going to form a close relationship even after the grumpy facial expression has disappeared. I do pay big attention to the first impression I get of a person because it tells a lot about someone even before he or she starts talking.

Psychology says that it takes just 90 seconds to get a first impression. In this short time the first information about the person is already written in your head and it's going to stay there for longer than you might think. In those 90 seconds, you just get to enter the room, greet someone or exchange a few polite phrases. The real conversation starts later, but the first impression can already be strong enough to show if investing time in interaction with you is promising, desirable or just a waste of time. A good first impression can give you a nice start at a new job, when closing a good deal, selling something or winning a competition, but if you leave a bad first impression, you're drowning yourself by cutting your possible success rate.

In those first seconds you appear in front of someone, nobody can see the depth of your beautiful personality and nobody can figure out that you truly have a bright mind. What they can see is how you look, what you wear, how you move and how you talk. Joe The Baker might be a truly fun and great personality with a kind heart, but if he looks insecure and talks with uncertainty when meeting his potential employer for the first time, he might stay behind the door when it's time to choose the best option between 10 people. Your skills matter, but so many times I've seen employers who are in doubt and struggle choosing between a person with an average resume and good first impression and another with stunning skills and professional qualities but whose facial expressions, manner of talking and gestures simply push you away. Big and small businesses, which really care for their business development and their employees as well, truly pay attention to these small things. They know that value and success are in details.

To create a good first impression when going after your dream job, you have to look good, and it's not just about suitable outfit, your hairdo and matching colors. Your entire being is telling about you—your confidence, your relationships with yourself and the world around you. A natural smile is a truly necessary feature in your image. It can save the situation in case you are far from perfect and it can also be a great, warm and welcoming feature on your face.

If you smile, your face isn't the only thing that changes. A smile can be heard in your voice as well and it's important to have that positive voice. As the sound changes when you smile, the tone of your voice projects the positive feeling. In fact, if you close your eyes and listen to two different people talking—one without a smile and the other one happily smiling – you'll be able to recognize which one is smiling and which one isn't. The changes in our voices come from our inner feelings. When you talk with the positive feeling of smiling (even if smile isn't in your face while talking), everyone can detect it, and it puts you in the category of people that are nice to hear.

This is what your smile tells if it's a part of the first impression:

- You are happy to be where you are. It's simply easier and more pleasure to interact with people who are excited to interact.

- You are confident. As we discussed previously—it tells about your positive mindset and confidence about your skills. Any skill that comes with confidence has more power and value than a skill you use without confidence.

- You are friendly. There is always a green light for friendliness, because it also is a sign of honesty.

- You have a positive mindset—that's the winner's mindset in all situations.

These are the core qualities the smile ties to your personality while forming a first impression. You need all of them if you're willing to develop professionally and move on to reach "open waters." Also, do not over-smile as you do not want to be seen as an overly confident person. It's always important to find the right balance using common sense!

What first impression do you leave? You can ask some co-workers or friends what their first impression was when they first met you. They might not remember if you left neutral first impression, but they will surely remember if it was explicitly good or bad. Still remember what we discussed about faking and mimicking smiles? It's worth it to get into experiments and exercises with mimicking and faking to develop a good first impression and present yourself in a positive manner always and forever. Wherever you go, whatever you do and whomever you meet, the first impression truly counts. By leaving a good first impression you are creating positive self-image what encourages positive reaction from others directed your way.

Smile simply makes you look like a person others want to relate to. It makes you more appealing and approachable. If you want to present yourself in a positive manner, don't forget to put on the most beautiful accessory—your smile.

• Smile to Become a Good Leader

Not all of us have natural leadership skills, but that's something that is highly valued in society and job market. Leadership skills aren't beneficial only for managing and leading groups of people. A good leader in every level of organization brings in development, productivity and motivation, but it also helps on a personal level. If you are seen as a person with leadership skills you are seen as the one who is able to lead yourself—motivate, increase productivity and reach goals. If career, professional development or your own private business is something that matters to you, presenting your good leadership skills might be a good advantage in your life.

If you don't have or haven't developed your leadership skills, no worries—all individuals in a successfully organized society or team don't have to be leaders and leaders are not needed in all jobs, but nothing is worse than showing that you might be a wicked leader: insecure, unable to support emotionally and lift the spirits of a group, stressful, lacking empathy and inner harmony and so on. Nobody wants to be around this person and most likely seeing the leader appearing somewhere around or even coming closer increases the stress levels and gives goose bumps to everyone who is supposed to follow him or her. Imagine how the person who has all these traits might look like! What's his or her casual facial expression? I bet smile isn't the first thing that comes to mind! Poor leaders are the ones who force others to follow them, but don't create in others the willingness to follow. People are chit-chatting about them in a negative manner, and there definitely is a reason for that.

A good leader

- is self-confident
- understands others
- is supportive and takes in account the ideas, complaints and comments of others
- can motivate and uplift the spirits of others
- doesn't push, but create the wish to follow

- doesn't give orders, but allows everyone to be involved so each person can find "What's in it for me?" while being on the way to bigger common goal
- is able to ask for help if needed and has humility
- is loved and respected by his or her subordinates

Of course, a good leader has to make decisions, clearly know what he or she is doing and set the direction things are going, but the leader doesn't always have to be the smartest person in the room. A good leader needs to be the person in charge, not the scary one behind the closed doors.

Imagine what the good leader looks like! What's his or her casual facial expression? What is that expression that makes others feel understood and supported? What's the expression of a self-confident person who can encourage, help and show the way? What do leading people we love and appreciate look like? They are the ones who have smiles on their faces. I haven't seen a good leader without a smile, and I believe it's impossible to be a good leader if your subordinates never get a smile from you and can't share it with you.

By the way, I believe every good teacher should be a positive leader—someone students are willing to follow and learn from. I can assure that students would be more attracted to you and the subject you teach if you, as a teacher, smiled more. You see, shared smiles always come back. Smiles do not just leave you and disappear in thin air. They are coming back to you in different forms of positivity. If you are a teacher (or, for example, just trying to teach something to your kids at home), do it with a smile—it won't hurt you and it can't cause any negative consequences.

Mahatma Gandhi (1869-1948)—the inspiring leader of Indian independence movement—said, "I suppose leadership at one time meant muscles; but today it means getting along with people." It's actually often quoted as a joke, but even if it's presented in a careless, joyous manner, it still perfectly captures the essence of what leadership is. If you lack leadership skills or you feel you aren't a good leader although you are required to lead others, start from the basics—learn to smile.

• Smile to Make Them Trust You

I don't use the services of shady companies even if they offer lower price. I don't buy things on the street from people who seem untrustworthy. I don't invite in my home people I don't trust. I want to be reliable and I want to have honest people in my life. I'm willing to deal with those I can count on, but some people simply don't leave the impression of being reliable, probably even against their own will. They just have THAT face... The face of a sales man that automatically switches on the alarm in our minds: "Be careful! That person might convince you to do something you don't want, buy something you don't need or give away something you can't afford to waste!" Salesmen in general aren't villains, but people are programmed in their minds to say "No" to solicitation. This is due to the courtesy of the many signs, advertisements, commercials and phone solicitations we have daily. People won't buy from a sales man anymore. They will buy from a friend. So, if it happens that you are a salesman or have some sort of similar occupation, how do you get friends with your clients? Be friendly and care about what they need, not what you need. Smile to greet them, make them feel important. People will make financial decision based on an emotional decision first. Do I like the person who sells? Do I trust him? Do I like what he offers me? In many cases, when friendly trust builds up between a client and a sales man, the client will buy from him and not from anyone else.

If I intuitively spot a fake smile that creates doubts about the reliability of a person, I step back and don't get into further deals with that person. If he doesn't display any emotion at all, it makes me suspicious—if you truly have a good product to sell, you usually don't stay indifferent to it. I'd rather see an awkward emotional display than no emotion at all. Indifference doesn't make me to trust in someone, while authenticity does the job.

If I see a genuine smile, I know I can trust the person. If I feel that the person who is desperately trying to fake a smile has the best intentions, I'll trust—I'll deal with that person, find out what he or she has for me, listen and probably even buy from that person. You might not be aware of it, but you do exactly the same. Intuitively you feel if you can trust the person or not. Unfortunately, majority of us are masters of ignoring our own intuition.

Business uses smiling as a tool to create trust. You'd trust a smiling person more. Whenever you have the choice, you'll go with the smiling person. An ice-cream seller on the street corner will sell more if he smiles. A person who's trying to collect donations for a dog shelter will get more if he smiles.

Nobody would smile in product commercials on TV if smiles didn't make the advertised products look more reliable and didn't shape your cravings for the same satisfaction. To be honest, I really don't mind that my money goes where smiles are shared.

Just like smiles of others make you trust someone, your smile can make others trust in you. If you want to get more deals, sell more, get more collaborations, and hear more "Yes!" answers to your requests, put a smile on your face. If you want people listening to you, smile. If you want to get a positive feedback and hear people talking about you, your products or services in a positive manner, you have to share positivity with others as well. If you don't hand out positivity, the person you are dealing with simply doesn't have it to share further with others, including you. It's like a leaflet: if you give it to someone, he or she will have the information.

Of course, you can't just smile and promise without giving. You have to give as well, keep your promises and deliver the best you can, but don't forget that not just people, but also their money, love going the direction where they can receive and enjoy positivity in any form. A smile is a great expression of satisfaction and pleasure, and when you smile, you are encouraging others to feel the same about you and whatever you are giving. The most important task in sales is being genuine and caring about your client. In your mind, do what's good for them even if you'll lose a sale. You might lose it now, but you'll gain it and even more later on their referrals. Smile and care, the rest will follow.

There's another interesting study from 1995 that suggests that smiles don't only create trust, but also help us to get judged lighter when we have done something wrong.[7] By showing the pictures of a female with different smiles (felt smile, false smile and miserable smile) and non-smiling neutral facial expression, Marianne LaFrance and Marvin A. Hecht from Boston College investigated the difference in how smiling and non-smiling transgressors are judged. The study showed that it doesn't matter what kind of a smile decorates person's face, what matters is that smiling people are judged with more leniency. While smiling people aren't perceived as less guilty, they get more mercy. Smiling people look better, friendlier and more appealing, but as this research suggests, the main thing that makes smiling transgressors receive more leniency is that they seem more trustworthy. Got in trouble? Smile! Made a mistake? Try smiling while explaining to your boss what happened, even if that's a miserable smile in your face—it's better than no smile at all! Smile in your face creates trust in you, and being seen as a trustworthy person truly helps in many situations!

Your business can grow from smiles. Your career can develop if you share smiles. New collaborations and professional success will follow your smile. And even if you care just about getting paychecks, try to work for those paychecks with a smile on your face and see how your work-life changes!

9

Smile for Love

"When I saw you I fell in love, and you smiled because you knew."
–Arrigo Boito, Italian poet and librettist

A simple smile can start beautiful friendships and relationships that are based on love. A simple smile can bring peace in conflict situations. It can significantly improve relationships that have gone wrong and change communication with others. It transforms interactions because anger and negative energy lose power in front of a warm, genuine smile. The smile is mightier than the sword.

The transformative power of smiling might sound like a very romantic statement, but these aren't just words taken out of the blue. Traveling around the world, interacting with huge audiences and analyzing personal relationships, I've got a lot of proof of its immense power. You really can feel like a magician when you discover that you have such an amazing power within you—the power of smile. We all have it and we all can use it to transform our relationships.

• Smile to Connect and Strengthen Your Bonds

Having fun together creates positive memories. Sharing positively charged moments with others makes others see us in a positive light. If we can feel good together, we simply don't think anything bad about each other. If smiles create trust between people, they also help people to get closer and strengthen their bonds.

That's a pretty common situation: two people who once were madly in love and seemed the most compatible people on earth a few years later become estranged. They are still together as a couple, but something is missing there... At the beginning when people fall in love they are excited, they do many things together to discover each other and they are also trying to show the best of themselves, so they smile often and respond with smiles even to unfunny jokes and awkward situations. Later people get used to each other's company so much that they stop trying to show the best of themselves. They honestly respond to unfunny jokes, and many things that seemed funny or sweet earlier start getting annoying and simply too ordinary to react to them through any emotional display. They don't share smiles that often. They stop caring about making the other feel good every day. They are drifting apart and start looking for joy and happy feelings somewhere outside of their relationships. It's still good for them to be together since they both have the feeling of safety, but that missing part is making the ditch between them to grow bigger. Sometimes people simply don't notice how it happens, but one day they wake up with the revelation that they are becoming strangers to someone they once truly loved and with whom they enjoyed every moment being together.

So, they decide to save their relationships—it's a big job that requires efforts and time. What works for one couple, doesn't suit the other one: as individuals we are different, but also couples and relationships aren't all built the same way. Solving relationship issues is a delicate thing that depends on the situation and involved sides, but there is one small thing that can help all couples. Sharing smiles and responding with smiles can ease conflict, bring peace, encourage bonding and strengthen the bonds of each relationship. While a smile alone isn't a solution for complicated relationship issues, it's an ice-breaker that can help on the way to healed connections.

A 2015 study conducted by Belinda Campos at University of California, showed that smiling is an important part of any short and long-term relationship.[8] Taking in account that positive emotional displays are signs of cooperation and acceptance, the research team tested the role of the positive emotions in relationships. First, they tested 66 dating couples to check how aware they are of each other's positive emotions. The second experiment tested if positive emotions help form and strengthen social bonds. For the second experiment, 91 women watched emotional film clips accompanied by a stranger or a roommate.

It might seem logical that the better you know a person,

the easier it is to perceive his or her emotions, but the study showed that even people who don't know each other for a long time are able to perceive positive emotions pretty accurately. The second experiment proved that people were more attracted to and felt closer to strangers who showed positive emotions. They discovered that people perceive each other's positive emotions much better than negative ones, and those positive emotional displays, especially broad Duchenne smiles, strengthen connections between people. This study shows that smiling is an important part of any relationship because smiles are signs of our openness to cooperate; they display our affection and acceptance and also make others trust us and feel safe together.

Cooperation, acceptance, affection, trust and the sense of security—isn't that what we all want from relationships? Isn't that exactly what a successful, happy relationship is? Smile to dissolve negativity, smile to get balanced and use smile to form and strengthen your bonds with others. Learn to smile for love! Also, always remember that smiling is contagious—if your partner doesn't seem very keen on sharing smiles, help them by sharing your smile! If he or she catches your smile and lets the healing power of smiling into themselves, they will also be able to open up to form a closer and stronger relationship with you! This is the most underrated key to successful long-term relationships. Now you have this key—use it!

You can start new relationships with a smile. You can nurture your relationships with it daily. You can also revive and renew your relationships by letting your significant other see your smile. Don't let the words "I love you" out of your mouth without the expression of positive emotions in your face! Do not allow "Goodnight" or "Good morning" become just words without real emotional value. Say "Please" and "Thank You" with a smile on your face. Everything you say can reach the other person like a random sound—like a cat's meow on the street—or it can reach the other person along with your positive energy. Which option would trigger a genuinely positive response?

Remember also that smiles sometimes say more than words. If you make eye contact, your smile will be perceived and will create positive response. When you approach someone with anger, you get anger, fear or disappointment in return. If you complain about someone and shame him or her, you can't expect them to share love and joy with you. When you are trying to keep smile on your face and in your heart while talking to another person, you are building a strong and happy bond between you both. You are creating comforting, love-based communication. There is nothing to learn and there are no secret underwater stones you could fall upon—just do it! Let your loved ones see your smile and share it with your partner, friends, family, colleagues, neighbors and others who participate in your life and fulfill your life with friendly connections. Whether they are long-lasting relationships or momentary transactions, we can make them enjoyable and positively charged.

There is one little exercise I recommend to any couple and which I also use a lot. It's very simple, but I when I came up with it and tried it, I found it to be very beneficial. It's a smiling exercise that brings people closer and opens them for positivity in relationships. Here is what you have to do:

1. Sit in front of your partner. Make sure it is a relaxed environment, without distractions. You may sit on two chairs in front of each other (no table in between), on the floor on a comfy pillow, or even on bed. The goal is to sit in front of each other with a close distance that if you wish you could hold each other's hand.

2. Sit straight, close your eyes and smile for 30 seconds. Breathe deeply in and exhale slowly, in a comfortable, relaxing pace. In these 30 seconds think only about positive things you are grateful for in your relationship with a person sitting in front of you.

3. After 30 seconds, open your eyes and look at your partner's face. Discover the face that make you smile. Keep the smile and keep the positive thoughts. Think your best thoughts and without saying a word look into your partner's eyes, let him or her feel all the positivity that you have. Let them do the same to you and while you think your happy thoughts, embrace the happiness in their face. Keep the eye contact for approximately 30 seconds, while keeping your breathing at a relaxing pace.

4. After about a minute, close your eyes again and let your positive thoughts sink into your body parts. Think about any happy situation that comes in your mind and the thoughts you felt for your partner. Picture it all, imagine it and feel it in you. Keep the smile on your face while breathing at the same speed. Keep your eyes closed for about 30 seconds.

5. Open your eyes, look at your partner with the same positive smile and give them a hug. Keep this hug for approximately 30 seconds. Feel the energy and love passing between you both. Let the positivity transfer from one to another.

This exercise is very beneficial if repeated few times a week. You can benefit if you decide to do it daily or weekly as well. These few minutes of a mindful pause together with your partner is a little thing, yet a powerful couple smiling meditation that will diffuse any stress and embrace your connection to your significant one.

Try it, do not be afraid, teach your partner and experience it together. You will only understand the benefit after you have tried it.

• Smile to Bring Peace

Arguments and conflicts are natural in all kinds of relationships. When two or more people meet and try to make their lives together, build a business, have fun or support someone else together, they do not always agree on everything. Each of them might have different standards, ambitions and ideas of how things should work, and that's just normal. Arguments often bring out truths and help us figure out the future together, but do they have to be aggressive and leave us with bitterness afterwards? It's a huge NO!

This reminds me of an English proverb: "You can't make an omelet without breaking eggs." Some arguments really break something into us, but it doesn't mean that you have to react to it like a drama queen. Are you sad that you have to break eggs for an omelet? Are you madly screaming while cooking that omelet? Normally, no, because you know why you are doing it–to get something better than it is now–food, nutrition and satisfaction. Is it hard to acknowledge that arguments happen exactly for the same reason? We argue because something doesn't feel good to us and we know we could make it better. We argue because we care. If we wouldn't care we would not bother putting our time and energy into such unpleasant action.

I'm trying to say that you don't have to bring simple disagreements to boiling conflicts. You don't have to go to war against other people, because in every war there is only loss. Sometimes we want to prevent getting into conflicts or wars, and in some cases all we do is waste our precious energy and other resources thinking and planning how we can win, forgetting that in order for us to win, the other side must lose. For a moment, you might be satisfied about winning an argument with a friend, but will it make you happy if it leaves ugly marks in your friendship and makes your friend feel down? There is also a chance to make almost every argument a win–win situation for both involved sides.

You can stop conflicts and solve them without bitterness. I'm not telling that you should try to handle arguments with peace. I know that YOU CAN DO IT. I'm talking from my own experience: when you focus on positivity and accept it as a way to solve unpleasant situations, you have equipped yourself with strength. Aggression, offensiveness, accusing and insulting others in arguments is a weakness. The inability to solve conflicts with peace is a weakness. Smiling through unpleasant situations and doing your best to solve them with peace is a clear sign of a strong person in front of you, a person who is worth listening to. You can be that person who brings peace with your smile.

Some time ago together with my family I visited friends in Canada. We all decided to go to "Wonderland," an amusement park similar to Disneyland. Our teenage kids, of course, wanted to have fun apart from the smaller kids, so we just gave them the tickets and let them go. My friends had got the tickets from a website that offered a really good deal, but at the entrance it turned out that the tickets weren't valid. They were purchased on a fraudulent website. My friend's wife explained the situation to the administrator and asked what we can do now. The tickets were pretty expensive, so she asked maybe there is a chance of getting at least a discount, but they didn't want to let us in. Here we all were—9 people hoping for a joyful day together, but stuck at the entrance. Then the manager came and my friend had to explain everything again to another person. The situation wasn't going to be solved fast and the tension started to grow. It seemed that people around me were starting to go from angry to totally crazy, but my friend's wife was still smiling. Her husband was really upset and wanted to help getting involved in the conversations with the administration of the amusement park, but she healed him by saying, "Let me handle this." After an hour of difficult communication with the resort's administration, she was angry, but forced herself to smile. Then she turned to the manager and with a kind smile in her face said: "Listen, all we want is just to get in and enjoy the day. It's been already an hour arguing with you, but I'm still smiling. Maybe you can step back and let us in." The craziness of the situation disappeared, the solution was found. We were allowed to purchase the tickets at the same discounted rate the fraud website has sold them, instead of paying the full price and later my friends even got back the money they had spent on the fraud website. It all came to a successful ending on all sides due to patient, positive thinking and a smiling face. We were finally in, then she turned to her previously upset husband who was trying to solve the conflict with a negative mindset and in the heat of harsh emotions, and said, "See, when you smile everything gets resolved." He smiled and responded, "I just wanted to show you how NOT to react!" Ironically, he was right!

Before you get mad and resentful, ask yourself if that will solve anything. Usually, all it does is bring in unnecessary negativity that makes everything worse. I have witnessed conflicts solved with smiles and peace bring people closer, and they hug after an argument.

Don't be scared to say, "Sorry," if you acknowledge that you haven't been right. If you look someone in the eyes and say, "I'm sorry," no one can argue with that. A tiny smile of peace to follow may break the ice. Acknowledging and admitting a mistake takes more power than fighting, and it's sometimes the only truly beneficial solution. You don't have to always be right, and not all conflicts have to be solved by saying who has been right and wrong. Sometimes you need to think smart, not right.

First, write in your mind that arguments and conflicts aren't dangerous: they're not about saving yourself from decay and they aren't for announcing who is the winner. They happen to find the best solutions that would be acceptable for all involved sides. If you keep this in your mind, it will bring you peace in your manner of solving conflicts.

Second, remember the power that is sparkling within you and willing to express itself through you—your positivity that can be expressed through a simple smile. When you send out positivity, others can perceive it, and their aggression and anger loses power. When you come with genuine kindness, only the biggest villain can respond with hate. When you smile, peace finds the way to others. Your positivity needs a smile to get transferred. Remember about reflecting and mimicking expressions and emotions of others! You do it, and others are copying your emotional states as well. Use it for good! A simple smile can turn any argument from a disaster to a blessing.

• Smile to Make Others Feel Better

My father-in-law was an amazing man. Tough as a rock on the outside, but on the inside, gentle and soft. The man did not smile, and at times it was a bit intimidating to be with him as his face was always serious. I noticed that the only thing that made him smile was other people smiling around him, especially kids. He could not resist the smiles of kids as for him they were pure and innocent, so their smiles always came from the heart. (Can you stay serious in front of a smiling child? Their authenticity is so strong and honest that every person who has a loving heart would really have to try hard to resist them.) Later, I noticed that if I was smiling when I met my father-in-law, he'd smile back, and the energy in the room transformed from that moment on.

We can't help it. It's just happening naturally—reflecting and mimicking is a part of our subconscious that we are born with. When we feel danger, we get stressed and tense, and others can feel it and they reflect it. When we feel joy and happiness, we relax and smile. My father-in-law smiled more often as we visited him more and more. When we felt joy, it transferred to him too.

Smiling is contagious and it reflects back on each and every person surrounding you. They might not pay attention to it, but they definitely feel it. Smiling is an urge, a reflection of your feelings at that time. People don't even know when they smile, unless you point it out. Then they acknowledge it and notice their own smiles when they force them, and that's not always a bad thing. As you've read previously forced smiles are actually putting in action the same mechanism as genuine smiles. If you want to feel better, smile. If you want to make someone else feel better, share a smile with them.

There are times when deep talks, motivational phrases and comforting words are necessary, but nothing can replace a shared smile. We are sometimes obsessed by pushing our opinions on others and trying to teach them how to live better. We share inspirational quotes and deep thoughts we have read somewhere and often all it does is making ourselves feel smarter, but doesn't really help someone. You can support someone by listening and showing your understanding, but that's not always what people need. Sad people lack joy. Upset and depressed people need the feelings of happiness. Stressed people need laughter to turn away from problems and relax. Sometimes all they need is to raise their feel-good chemical levels! They need to smile, but can't find triggers for smiling in themselves. You can be the one who really helps. Share a smile and do what it takes to make your loved ones smile more! Tell jokes, watch comedy shows, ride a roller-coaster together, play funny games—the world is full of things you can do to make someone smile.

Your relationships with others hugely depend on the energy you give when interacting with them. You can complain that others are negatively minded, grumpy or sad, but you can also change it by changing the energy that comes out of you and reaches everyone around you.

When others mimic and reflect your positive emotional display—your smile—they are growing positivity together with you. They are transforming the mood of others around them as well. It's a chain you can start and help grow. You can save the day with your smile!

Let's help ourselves feel good! Let's start the chain reactions helping others feel better! We smile at them, they smile at us, they smile at others, others smile at them, others smile at others and it may go on and on and on.

10

Life Lessons from Kids

"If a child can't learn the way we teach, maybe we should teach the way they learn."
-Ignacio Estrada, teacher and grants administrator

Communication with kids is slightly different than communication between adults, that's why I don't want to ignore such a huge part of our daily lives. You don't have to be a parent, a teacher or a doctor to get involved in the lives of kids—your grandchildren, nieces, brothers and sisters, kids of your friends, neighborhood kids—they are everywhere around us testing us and learning from us on every corner. We live in the same world, yet their perceptions and actions put them in a dreamlike fairy-tale state where everything is big and the imagination is wild. There are many surprising and undiscovered things, but their emotions are clear and pure. When a child cries, the pain of the entire world is in that cry, but when you see kids smiling, it's a pure joy all over their faces. There's something we can relearn from them. They're small, but can remind us a lot about our basic functions and true nature.

If you smile at a child, you'll catch his or her attention. The child will look at you, come to you and respond to you. If you show a serious, grumpy or angry face, the child will turn away or maybe even start crying. Children are pure in their feelings and they perfectly feel the mood and openness of adults. Their analytic, conscious mind hasn't taken over them yet and they are more connected to their real feelings and intuitive mind than adults. They feel us and magnify their own feelings because their minds aren't stuffed with difficult thinking patterns, facts, ideas and knowledge that could suppress, overshadow and make them to ignore what they feel. Up to the age of 8, kids are more clairvoyant and open to their mystic, inner selves. Kids don't get into over-thinking, and in most cases will blurt out whatever comes from their feelings, the gut feeling and real emotion. Later, we start to get adjusted in our world and are molded by the knowledge our life experience gives us. Compared to a 5-year-old child, adults are pretty good at ignoring and disconnecting from their real feelings. We fear judgment, care about our looks, about how others will see us and what they will think about us. We control our emotions because it makes us feel in control of our lives.

While controlling your emotions is a good and beneficial skill in many situations, it can also do harm. If controlling your emotions becomes more important than understanding, accepting and, most importantly, living your emotions and following your heart, you are becoming disconnected from who you are and your open-mindedness can get lost in it. It's like losing a map that shows where your joy and happiness is. You just go with your logic and let analysis set the framework for you on what is acceptable to others and how you should feel. But how you should feel is often not how you actually feel. People get into relationships and marriages because they terribly want to be in relationship, because of peer pressure and what society expects them to do, not because the heart says, "Yes! It's for real!" People accept new jobs that elevate their statuses, but sometimes in moments of being alone and totally honest with themselves they discover that what they do isn't actually what they want to do. Some people even spend their entire lives working hard to get what others wish for them to have, what makes them look more successful, but not what they actually want. If you ignore the signals of your intuitive mind, you are at a risk of being dishonest with yourself and, of course, others as well. You might be able to explain why exactly you are doing something, but if your real feelings and emotions are pushed into the background you can disconnect from your inner world, which is actually built from positivity, love, peace and harmony.

All that kids care about is following the map to happiness. They go into world with open minds and they feel when adults around them are authentic and when they are fake. More than anything, however, they crave pleasure. When they acknowledge that they can also use specific emotional displays to get something they want, they start crying or smiling to manipulate adults around them—it all happens naturally and for the sake of getting what makes them happy.

In comparison, adults are attracted to pleasure and beauty as well, but they often say no to what they want in order to keep what they have—life in the comfort zone. I'm not saying you should give up the seriousness and importance of your adulthood, but some authenticity wouldn't hurt... If you followed the map of your happiness like kids do, you would change your world and really live the happiness. Children start smiling in the womb. They share smiles with people around them and smile while they sleep. They smile while playing with others and playing alone. They even share genuine smiles with their toys and with themselves. You were a child as well and you did it too, but as you grew up, things changed. "Adulthood isn't some kind of a joke," says a man in a suit, and pours himself a glass of whiskey to relax and just enjoy the evening. Then he meets a friend, they talk and laugh, joke and even make fun of each other. Some grumpy people say they behave like kids, but it doesn't disturb them—they're feeling good and they're not going to let anyone take these precious hours of ease from them. When the next working day comes, the man puts on his suit, checks his serious face in the mirror and walks out the door. He knows that the daily life of adulthood isn't joy, although it could be.

It's human nature to be happy, positive and enjoy our days walking on earth, diving into oceans, flying above the clouds, and simply being here now, enjoying the happiness that is within us instead of chasing it around. If we weren't naturally positive-minded, humanity wouldn't have survived so long. If we weren't naturally positive-minded, we wouldn't be attracted to positivity and love and wouldn't seek it around us. We restlessly seek happiness in all possible forms because we have forgotten that it is inside of us. Children do not acknowledge by conscious mind their superpowers of being happy, but they are happy. You can read it in their faces. Ask a child if he or she is happy! I won't tell you what a child might answer. Just ask and you will find it out!

Kids are connected to their natural source of happiness and they spread happiness around. Have you noticed that you smile more around kids? Now you know why: because they smile genuinely and you reflect their expressions. Observe kids to remember what it means to dream and enjoy, feel strong positive emotions and share them with others. This is what I used to do when I was younger and didn't have my own kids. Now I do have kids and I'm still doing it—not just giving to them, but also learning from them. The only thing that scares me when I look at them is that my kids grow so fast, and soon I won't have young kids anymore and will have to wait for my grandkids to come.

You've probably heard of connecting with your "inner child." I would call it connecting with your true nature. Whenever you have a chance, spend time with children and enjoy their company. For sure you can easily get tired of their enormous energy, but they'll also give you a positive emotional boost as you share smiles and are forced to get back to playfulness. Here's how I've learned from kids and what you can do to open your heart for authenticity and freedom of open-mindedness:

1) Check their reactions when they try to understand others.

Spend time with kids and try to check how they react to your positive and negative emotional displays. Smile, show surprise, sadness, seriousness and see how they respond. It will help you understand not just how kids see you, but how we all perceive and respond to each other. If adults have mastered their skills to hide and control their emotions, kids clearly show what actually happens in all of us on a basic level—it's pretty much the same for all human beings no matter how old we are. Checking how kids react to what you do or say will help you read adults emotions as well. The emotional display in kids and adults might not be exactly the same, but if you train your mind to see and recognize emotional displays in children, it'll help you read the emotions of adults.

2) Learn from child imagination.

Play with children and accept their rules. It doesn't mean doing and agreeing on everything they want, but simply playing the way they play. The main rule in their games is using your imagination.

When kids play, they let their imagination go wild and they fully believe in it. If a child is pretending to be "mommy" or "daddy," they do not pretend. They become who they are trying to imitate. And they can be everything—ballerinas, butterflies, frogs, cartoon characters—wherever their imagination can go. They build cities in sand without craving perfection, but rather enjoy the process. It's something adults should remember.

The reality around you is first created in your mind. When children play, they don't worry about things they don't have for the game. They use whatever is around them, and with the help of imagination, they create everything they need. A simple room becomes a palace, a blanket turns into flying carpet, a pencil can be used as a spoon and a pillow becomes a shield. The imagination takes their mind where they want to go. You can say that you wish to be successful, but you can also take the next step – allow your mind go where your happiness is. Happiness isn't just a word. See it, feel and explore it like kids do—be in it. Play kids' games in your adult life and create the reality you want for yourself! Smile like a kid and feel like one!

When interacting with kids, try to smile as much as you can—it'll make yourself feel better and it'll create a bond with the child and make the child feel good. Fake your smiles if they don't come naturally and smile genuinely to share joy with children. When you are interacting with adults, your gestures and expressions can get judged, while kids, who are in the process of discovering the world and learning how it works, are more open to people around them. Smile to test and to learn, and remember that enjoyment is essential for opening the gate to your own happiness!

A Smile for the Future

I wish everyone smiled more, and I believe that it could solve many problems we have in the world today. Unfortunately, while facing the world as it is and learning from people around us, we forget that smiling is our real superpower, and we smile less and less. In school programs, there's no place for learning the power of smile, but there's someone who can teach it to children—the people around them. Not just family members but everyone who interacts with them regularly is helping them learn these essential life skills. Grumpy people make kids grumpy. Aggressive people make kids release their own aggression. Kind people let kids see the power of kindness, and positive people help children develop a pattern for actions and reactions based on positivity.

Think about your childhood. What was the mood around you? What people were around you regularly? Do you have any close person that was your hero in childhood and why? Was there anyone you remember as a very positive person? What was your relationship with that person? Were you attracted to this person? Did anyone teach you about the power of a positive mindset by demonstrating it? Could you observe the power of positivity from your surroundings?

By sharing a smile with a child, you're encouraging that child to smile. It means, you're encouraging the child to feel happy and comfortable. You're triggering the brain behind the smile to release feel-good chemicals and regulate hormonal levels that allow that child to feel good. You can help any child instill in their minds the beneficial pattern that leads to searching for happiness and finding it within themselves. You can help a child grow up clearly observing and learning that talking while smiling, connecting with people with a smile and going through life troubles with a smile is the best and most beneficial way, and the child will do it and benefit from it for the rest of life! From the same beginning of a new life, you have the power to ensure that the child learns the skills that aren't destructive, but truly useful and helpful. And if there is a child in your life who can't learn it from his parents, you can still help by showing the child that there is another way to choose—the one filled with positivity.

Children learn from what they can observe and feel. Even if

they can't fully understand different emotions and problems of adulthood, they can still reach conclusions and recognize specific behavioral traits as powerful or useless. When the unconscious conclusion is made, it gets written into the mind and stays there waiting to be used. If children learn the power of smile in their childhood, as adults, they keep smiling more than those who haven't. The point is that everyone who interacts with any child could become the one to help a child learn to keep the positive mindset for the rest of their lives.

Children learn the most from what they observe, so, the best way to teach children some specific kind of behavior isn't by telling and discussing how it should be, but by being a good role model—showing by simply applying something in your own life. As teenagers, they start needing more words and talks (and most of them want and hate them at the same time), but children will learn more from what you do, not what you say.

The lessons kids learn at a young age stay with them the rest of their lives because in childhood the subconscious mind—which is very receptive—forms behavioral patterns that define their actions and reactions later in life. It's hard for adults to rewrite their minds and it requires intention and reinforcement, but for children it's much easier. Smiling and sharing smiles is a useful skill and a powerful tool that helps people succeed in their lives, form positive relationships and reach high professionally. Adults can teach kids to use this immense power for their own future benefit, and not by forcing them to smile and requiring them to smile, but by being role models and interacting with children with kindness and positivity.

We can teach our kids with smiles, give orders, explain things and answer their questions with smiles. We can show them how smiles bring benefits if we share them with everyone around us. We can also encourage kids to solve issues with smiles and live with a positive mindset. We can learn from them, enjoying and expressing positivity, and we can also give back by helping them keep this power for later in their lives. They'll probably forget how they learned it, and you won't get a credit for it, but you'd be helping more than just one person—you'd be helping everyone he or she comes in contact with.

Smiles spread in chains, and that's how you can become a part of one positive chain that keeps developing and spreading around the world. This is a way to volunteer that really makes the world a better place. From person to person, from group to group, from one generation to another one—that's how real change happens, not just on a personal level, but on a communal social level.

11

The Gateway to Authentic Smiling

"To be yourself in a world that is constantly trying to make you something else is the greatest accomplishment."
-Ralph Waldo Emerson, American essayist and poet

I don't want to you tell how many smiles per day you should share. I don't want you to walk around with a fake smile that simply looks creepy because I don't want anyone to feel inauthentic. I also don't want to tell you how many teeth you have to reveal smiling or how to fake a smile to look gorgeous in pictures. It's about cultivating a positive mindset and finding happy vibes that allow you to smile genuinely.

Genuine smiles come from genuine feelings. When you feel good, you radiate wellbeing and it's written on your face. Even if your mouth doesn't show a smile, it's there—in your eyes. The same happens when you're faking a smile—if it doesn't come from the heart, it's on your face—even behind a wide, bright smile can be sad eyes. Positive words or facial expressions sometimes can't hide the feelings inside you that contrast with what you're expressing. So, how can you smile genuinely if you don't feel like doing it? And how about people who are able to share genuine smiles even in biggest troubles and stressful situations? They're not super-humans, but there's something obviously different about them. They're nurturing a positive mindset—the one that brings a change in their lives and their faces. To smile for a change you have to learn to develop a positive mindset and open up to using and enjoying the power of your own smile.

You have already had some examples and exercises in this book for working on a positive mindset, and I hope you've tried at least a few of them. I also hope you're already enjoying the benefits of smiling, but before I let you go to explore the world filled with joy, success and happiness, it's important for you understand how to work with yourself to become that change—to smile more and attract all those benefits a smile can bring. For some people it's hard to fake a smile. For some people it's hard to remember in daily life how important smiling is, and others simply look at the power of smile as something magical, unexplainable and most likely—unreal. "The power of smile?" they would say. "Oh, yes, sure! Try paying your bills with a smile!" Well, if I went to pay my electricity bill hoping to do it with a smile alone I'm pretty sure it really wouldn't work—it's not like having a fairytale magic stick that you just wave it and everything happens immediately—but I'm pretty sure that I actually am paying my bills because of my positivity. Yes, you go and pay your electricity bills, but, hey, doing it and being able to do it is much better than paying your health bills! In any case you will need to pay bills for things you buy and services you use, but isn't it better to pay for it and feel wonderful?

Yes, my smile has brought me where I am now and it's helped me get great earning opportunities. My skills truly matter, but if I didn't have this positive mindset, I wouldn't see any chance to use my skills. Smiling actually is paying a big part of my bills while also opening doors to new opportunities. That's also how I want you to think about your life. That's what I want you to acknowledge, reach, experience and enjoy. If it doesn't work like that in your life now, there's a wall between your conscious and subconscious mind. No worries, everyone has this wall, it's called the critical factor and it is a gate protecting unwanted information from getting into the subconscious. So, in order to get the good things in you need to trick your own mind so the gate will open and the information will pass. Tricking your subconscious mind for positive things is good—it brings good things into your life. Taking life, and saying that everything is bad... Where would that bring you?

Your thoughts have to find the gateway to any changes you want to make in your life. We're not talking about magic now. It's about human psychology—how we grow, develop, accept and reject thoughts and ideas, behavioral patterns and reactions on a mental level.

Manipulating for Positive Thoughts

You know that life doesn't go the way you want it every day. It doesn't matter how rich, beautiful or successful you are—we all have our good and bad days. Also, the fact that you don't have something you want or need doesn't need to have a depressive influence on you. It's a matter of perception, and this is what you have to train to find the happiness that'll allow you to smile genuinely, not just in overwhelmingly positively situations, but through every ordinary day of your life.

Your conscious mind is doubtful, careful and always suspicious—it analyzes the information you get and separates fantasy from reality. Your subconscious mind is open and receptive, it's ready to accept new ideas and make you act accordingly to new realities. The subconscious mind doesn't separate fiction from reality. So, if you let new ideas in your subconscious mind, your conscious mind and behavior will change as well: if you let ideas into your subconscious mind, it has the tendency to accept and believe in them. Since the subconscious mind is gullible, it will absorb things and make a new reality out of them. This means that in order to be present in your daily life, positivity has to be seeded in your subconscious mind. However, it has to get through the control of your conscious mind first. When your subconscious mind is set on looking for positivity, nothing can stop you from sharing genuine smiles.

Happiness isn't a gift. It's a skill you can learn and develop, and even if you feel unhappy in life, you can work on it and achieve real happiness before you get all the other things that you think are necessary for being happy. Your mindset is the only thing that truly matters when it comes to how you feel in this world. If you have a negative mindset, winning a million in a lottery won't save you—it might give you an adrenaline rush for a while, but not lasting happiness. You need to pass the information of keeping positive mindset into your subconscious mind. Once positivity is rooted in your subconscious mind, you don't have to push yourself to look for happiness and positive vibes—you just have them inside whatever happens and you smile genuinely. Bad days will happen, but they won't make you unhappy—it's worthwhile to work on that!

You have probably heard about affirmations that are used to program new ideas into one's mind. You chose affirmative statement that you want to become true and repeat it to yourself again and again, until your mind fully believes in it and starts acting according to the idea you have. It's not as difficult as it sounds. If you told yourself every day that you're getting better and you feel better, your mind will make you act accordingly. So yes, you really will feel better. As your mind believes in something it acts according to the belief. If you have learned and believe that long exposure to the sun can cause sunburns, you will try to protect yourself—it comes naturally, because you know what you have to do. It's clear, right? If you truly believe that you're getting better after a sickness, you'll get better. If your mood is a 5 out of 10, you can still convince yourself and others that it is 10—and, yes, as your subconscious mind receives this idea, you really get there.

If you tell yourself you can fly like a bird just by waving your hands... well, your conscious mind blocks this idea—it's unrealistic, so, it isn't useful because it clearly is far from reality. If you are trying to plant in your mind an unrealistic idea that doesn't have any relation to your current reality, you're just creating a hole between your reality and wishes. When you set unrealistic goals for yourself, your thoughts and ideas are immediately rejected by the gateway that protects your subconscious mind. If you feel not the best, tell yourself, "I am healthy." "Healthy" is a mindset that your body and mind know and remember, so getting there is a realistic goal. If you tell yourself you're going to FLY like a superman, your mind knows that you can't and never did, so the conscious mind will block your idea and it will be rejected and won't even be considered. Always give yourself realistic goals, those that can be tangible and are within reach or those that your mind can recognize as a feeling from the past or an amplified feeling of the past. For example, "I'm earning 20 million dollars today" may be rejected to most. But if you say you will be earning $200 or $2000, it is realistic, depending on your usual income. Success and happiness are earned, but most also can be manifested. Negativity is what will pull you down, while working on developing positivity is the fun part—manifesting feelings and thoughts is free and can only bring good.

The critical factor (the gateway to the subconscious mind) is always there. It's there to protect us from thoughts and ideas that penetrate the subconscious. Otherwise, everything would be accepted as reality and our reality would be completely altered. However, there are a few things that can allow new thoughts and ideas to enter the subconscious. One of the ways to get something new in your mind is through misdirection—a method used in hypnotherapy in order to misdirect the mind, to open the gateway to the subconscious mind and start a conversation that results in acceptance of new ideas, changing our views, feelings or emotions on some of our issues. Another way is getting new ideas in your mind when the conscious mind is a bit tired and not fully in action, for example, right before falling asleep or just after waking up. In these times, the critical factor gateway has some openings, so it's easier to bring something new into your subconscious. There's a third way to go as well: repetition. When we repeat something to ourselves again and again, there'll be a point when the subconscious mind starts hearing it. Repetition gets the attention of the subconscious, so the more you repeat the ideas you want for your life changes, the bigger the chance for getting these ideas past the gateway and accepted as true.

Don't lie to yourself to keep a positive mindset, but remind yourself to look for positive aspects of every situation instead of trying to make things look worse than they really are. Remind yourself how much better you feel surrounded by peaceful and positive people than with depressed, stressed and always negatively minded people, and be that person. Allow yourself to be that person you can enjoy, allow yourself to be happy—sometimes all we need is permission... from ourselves. Don't tell yourself you're unhappy, stupid, ugly or unsuccessful because the more you repeat it to yourself, the more likely it is to because a self-made reality. The same mechanism works with positive messages. Allow yourself to show positive emotions. Don't reject them when they're present. Welcome positivity in your life and it will unlock your genuine smiling. You just have to install a positive mindset;

reasonable wishes and reminders will form a new path for your mind to follow. Belief is the gateway to success—no matter what you do. If you believe in something, you gain confidence in doing it and it becomes natural to you. Then there's just one thing to do to make positivity take strong root in your mind—work on your positive mindset and repeat it again and again. Repetition will strengthen your positive mindset making it a natural part of your day. Whatever happens, you can tell yourself, "I am healthy, I am peace, I am happy, I am good, I am whole and complete." These messages are projecting positivity, but not in an extreme line that would be rejected. You have to find positive statements to repeat, positive messages to get into your subconscious mind where they can turn into beliefs that define your actions. When an idea becomes your belief, this belief creates respective symptoms.

Just remember these 3 stages through which positivity has to get through to become a part of your daily life:

Conscious Mind	The Gateway	Subconscious Mind
• Careful, doubtful, • Analyzes Information, • Makes decisions, • Separates fantasy from reality, • Guards your subconscious	• A part of conscious mind that decides which ideas can pass into subconscious. • Protects the subconscious from overload of information that it doesn't need.	• Receptive, • Accepts ideas as reality • Operates all unconscious, automatic actions, • Holds our emotions and memories

from saving things in your mind as patterns or beliefs.	• Allows new ideas, knowledge, thoughts and revelations get into the subconscious where they become beliefs and form behavioral patterns.	from the very first day.

• Smiling Eyes Exercise

Before you move on in this book, I want you to see the difference your mindset makes. When you have proved the difference to yourself, it gets easier to accept and involve what makes you feel better. A smile can involve your entire face, but if the genuineness is lacking in your eyes, your smile has just a half of its potential. Those "smiling eyes" project your happiness and they come from your mindset.

You only need a mirror for this exercise.

1. Look at your reflection in the mirror for a few seconds—just your face. Smile at yourself like you would smile for a picture. If you wish, take a picture of yourself!

2. Close your eyes. Think about something that always makes you happy. Dwell upon a cheerful memory, a happy moment in your life—remember it and let it

charge you with positivity. We spoke about it previously in the book, so I hope you already know what to do here! You can also repeat to yourself a positive, comforting statement like, "I am peace. I am happiness. I am harmony." Check what charges you with positivity and let it inside your body—feel it!

3. Open your eyes and look into the mirror again. What do you see in the mirror now? How do you feel looking at your reflection now?

4. Take another picture of yourself and compare both pictures. What's the difference between the face you saw in the mirror before closing your eyes and after opening them again? Do you see what is meant by "smiling eyes"? What actually made the difference?

Let's make it clear—that magic that changed your face without physically changing was created by you, inside of you. As you allowed yourself to dwell upon happy, comforting thoughts, your mindset was charged with positivity—it invited the natural chemist in your brain to start working. This positivity is changing the way you are presenting yourself, the way you feel in the world and perceive it, and it also changes your communication with everyone around you because not just on physical levels, but also mental and spiritual ones, you send out a positive message. As you get positive mindset, your smile becomes genuine—truly life changing.

If you're struggling with a negative mindset and have to work on installing a positive one, don't forget this simple exercise! Try it again and again. It costs nothing, but has value you can't measure. Practice it to install a positive mindset and it will send a smile to your face more often!

Transform a Bad Moment in a Good One

No matter how positive you are, life has its manipulative way of turning moments upside down. However, it's up to us to accept or reject it. After all, it is OUR life! If positivity and happiness is your goal, you need to make sure you turn down any negative offer from life and whenever possible, transform it to a good, positive opportunity. Although life sometimes seems stronger and faster than we are, we can take lemons and make them into delicious lemonade.

Below are a few simple techniques—three methods I use when darkness strikes me and I want to bring light and love back to my life. For some, it might sound like a cliché, but trust me, tricks should not be used only in card magic, but also to trick our mind and gain back the feeling that we want to have. It's about how you see the world and not always about how the world is around you.

1. Close your eyes and stop your stressful moment. Picture a place where you've been before, a place that really made you feel calm. It may be a sunny beach, somewhere out in a green, lush field or anywhere else that resembles happiness in your heart. Be there, see it and take few deep breaths. Inhale, feeling how this peaceful place gets in your body and your mind. Push away any other thought for

that moment of visualization. As soon as you start feeling it, smile and let your face and body express that feeling. Encore this moment, so when you want to get back to it, you only need to smile, and that picture will pop into your mind.

Encoring means storing in your mind the feeling you want to have, and linking it to a trigger so you can access it whenever you want. Here, the peaceful place that you think of becomes a trigger for the good feeling. When you encore this in your mind for a minute, reaching and really feeling the happiness in your face, the next time you think of the same place, the beach smile will just rise as magic. You encore the feeling and trigger it when you think of the location or anything else you may choose!

2. When you feel stressed or stuck in a loop of worries, stop and take a cold glass of water. Drink it slowly and feel how the cold fulfills your body. Link that cold feeling to happiness, freshness and positivity. Feel how physically it is entering and calming your whole self—like a devastating, burning fire is extinguished by refreshing rain. As soon as you feel it, share the feeling on your face and in your body—feel relaxed, feel the cold water as if it resembles the happiness in that moment and positivity you need. When you feel it, express this feeling through your entire body, and the genuine happy smile will appear on your face. Encore that moment of happiness and peace for the

future, and recall it with a glass of cold water whenever you need to.

3. There are two ways to look at life: the half-full cup or the half-empty cup. The choice is up to you—according to which half of the cup you live your life. Can you guess what I prefer? You're right... always full! Despite extreme tragic situations, no matter how discouraging your day is, many others would exchange with you without even blinking. What I am trying to say, your case is not as bad as you think it is, and you might want to think of others that are less fortunate and would gladly take your place and be happy with it. So, taking things in proportion, knowing that much worse exists and that your situation is not as bad as you think. See the beauty in every wrinkle and the light in darkness. Always think of how fortunate you are despite your previous attitude. Think how lucky you are to be in this moment, in your own life. Close your eyes and feel it. Be in this moment and cherish it. Make it your own and reflect it on your body and face.

If you are upset and lack energy, stop pitying yourself. Close your eyes and charge yourself with positivity using any of these techniques. If you are stressed or tired, close your eyes to recharge. If you lack feelings of inner comfort, now you know what to do.

12

Learn About Yourself. Who am I?

"Yesterday I was clever, so I wanted to change the world.
Today I am wise, so I am changing myself."
–Rumi, Persian poet and Sufi mystic

"Just smile! Be happy!"–sounds easy, but is it? It actually is easy if you've convinced yourself that it is. I've heard people saying, "I just can't smile because I don't feel happy..." Not that often I hear someone saying, "My happiness depends only on myself." This is what I want you to understand–that your happiness is in your own hands.

To change your mindset and start enjoying a life filled with positivity, you need to recognize the holes in which your happiness falls, not being able to reach your everyday life. How much do you know yourself? Let me give you some tools that will enable you to test yourself and know better who you are.

No one is responsible for your happiness. Your girlfriend left you? You failed the test? They fired you from work? Or maybe you just have a mixed emotional day? That's okay, it happens to everyone, but don't blame your unhappiness on that situation, your boss, girlfriend, teacher or the grocery man. Happiness is in your hands and your hands only. You decide when you are happy. You decide when you are sad. Yes, we are influenced by outsourced situations, as we all are surrounded by dynamic life, but how we observe that life and absorb it into our psyche is our own decision. We can let life take us in a leash, or we can turn the situation and take life by the leash. Having the control in your own hands will give you the power to steer your way into a better life, into wellbeing and happiness.

Reflecting on who we are and how we feel is often all we need to see what is actually happening with us and start moving towards change. It's better to stop once to look into yourself and learn who you are than to walk around blind to your happiness for years.

Please answer this question:

If you would summarize your persona in two lines, what would they be?

Are you a happy person? Unhappy or sad? Kindhearted, friendly or reserved? Self-centered, fun loving or serious? Lone wolf or party animal? Take your time to work out this short description of yourself! It's just for you to learn who you are and how you perceive yourself. Don't write there what you would want others to say about you, but be honest: just two lines describing who you are.

• Test your mindset

Let's see the areas of your mind that crave improvement. When you know where the problem is, you can identify and catch it. You can work on changing specific traits.

The test is easy, but don't fool yourself. Face the reality and give honest answers. Nobody has to see your answers if you are not willing to share them, so, be honest with yourself while rating how much each statement complies with your personality. It'll help you lighten the darkest corners of your mindset, and learn and grow. Don't hurry, but also don't spend too much of time on each question to prevent overthinking. Taking a minute to answer each of the following questions should be enough.

All you have to do is rate your casual actions, behavior, expressions on the scale from 1 to 10 where 1 is the lowest and 10 the highest. For example, if the statement is, "I'm a happy person," 1 would mean you're terribly unhappy, but 10 that you consider yourself an absolutely happy person. The statements are divided in two sections. Rate how much you agree with each statement on the scale from 1 to 10, where 1 means, "I don't agree," and 10 means, "I fully agree with the statement." These are general questions to answer; don't just look at your latest life events, but your personality in general. Write in the box the numbers you get for each statement, so you can sum them up and reflect on your results later.

Positive statements:

I'm a happy person.	
I often make others laugh.	
I smile when I'm happy.	
I smile while I'm alone.	
I'm an outgoing person.	
I'm a relaxed person.	
I consider myself an optimistic person.	
When I'm with others I often smile.	
I often engage into activities that make me smile or laugh.	
I have my own healthy ways to get rid of stress.	
I take a good care of myself because I acknowledge that my happiness depends only on myself.	
I sometimes fake smiling.	
I sometimes smile just to make others feel better.	
I enjoy and try to enjoy my life every day.	
I smile every day.	

Negative statements:

I consider myself a negative-minded person.	
I often feel angry.	
I am a sad person.	
I never smile while I'm alone.	
I often complain.	

I'm a doubtful person. I find it hard to trust new people and ideas.	
I often feel stressed and anxious.	
When I'm with others, I usually don't show my emotions.	
When I'm with others, usually my facial expression is serious, sad or neutral.	
I often see many obstacles and problems before I can see the successful result.	
I don't laugh watching funny movies or hearing jokes.	
I don't fake smiling to create positive impression or make someone feel better.	
I often feel powerless and weak.	
I've never tried to use a smile to change any situation.	
I'm typically not a smiling person.	

The minimum points you can get in each section is 15 (if you have 1 for each statement) and the maximum 150 (if you have 10 for each statement).

How many points did you get from 15 positive statements and 15 negative statements? Sum them up separately in each section! Where did you get a higher score: in the section of positive or negative statements?

It'll be really beneficial for you if you reached a high score in the section of positive statements. I know, we are not getting very deep into your mindset now, but it can help you get the picture of it and see if it's positive or negative.

If you've reached 100 and more points on positive statements and have less than 50 points on negative statements, you are on the right way, so, keep going. If you haven't discovered the power of smile yet, you're about to discovering it very soon—a positive mindset will lead you to the experience and knowledge that allows you to make real changes with smiles.

Just take a look at the positive statements you rated with lowest numbers and try to work on increasing these numbers. They won't be raised right away, and your answer might be slightly different depending on your mood and the latest events in your life, but if you put some efforts into making yourself a more positively minded person, it will happen and you will share smiles more often. For example if you got 6 on, "I smile when I'm alone," make sure you can increase this number and start smiling more when alone and with other people. If you got 7 on, "I'm a relaxed person," work on finding more ways to become more relaxed and get rid of stress, and maybe try increasing this number to 8 or 9. Always think: what can make me feel even better?

But what can you do if you have high results on negative statements? Up to 50 is totally fine—we all are on a journey and we all have something to work out, but if you have got more than 100 on negative statements, your mindset is clearly negative. You are not helping yourself by maintaining such a negative mindset. You are blocking the power of smile that could be your superpower in everyday life. It won't be enough to just read this book. You need to practice what you read here, engage in experiments and get experiences that your mind will accept as proof of the power of smile and allow all of this to establish roots in your subconscious. Before you even practice, make yourself believe in the positive power.

Think about it like this: the way you make your bed is the way you will sleep in it. If you set your day in a positive way, your day will tend to be more positive because that's the tone that you've given it and it will manifest and influence all around you. This will bring a smile on your face that'll distribute your happiness, first within yourself and then circulating to others to create what you feel inside.

Each of these negative statements can become a positive statement about you that you can fully agree with. Each of these negative statements can disappear from the description of your personality, if you work on it. Always think about it this way—if you have a negative thought, stop, identify it and tell yourself: how would I want to feel? If you've identified your negative thought as "stressed," close your eyes and ask yourself: "Do I want to feel stressed? How would I want to feel instead?" Then give yourself the opposite, tell yourself that you feel comfortable and happy: it might be "relaxed," "happy", "stable," or any other feeling you want to have. Then ask yourself: "What will make me feel even better?" and think about what the visual thing or feeling is that you may think of which makes you feel even better than relaxed or happy. Always strive for the ultimate that will make you feel positive. Embrace it with a relaxed facial expression or a smile; it will help change your mindset and get you where you want to be.

Here are few examples of how to change your mindset with positive reinforcement.

1. "I consider myself a negative-minded person," can become, "I'm a positive-minded person." Nothing is purely bad and purely negative. You have to learn to

see good, expect good and notice positive things around you and inside of you. Count your blessings, write down three good things about your day before you go to bed, notice when negative thoughts are taking over and stop them, disarm them by showing yourself the positive and you can slowly become a truly positive-minded person.

2. "I often feel angry," could change to, "I'm a relaxed person," if you changed the way you look at things. That's exactly why we have this popular idiom: the devil is not so black as he's painted. Anger can't take over you if you don't allow it to grow. A single positive thought can stop it. Relaxation, exercises for stress reduction and learning to zoom out to see how big the problem is that makes you angry really could help. When you let the positivity spread to you, anger, fears and many troubles simply go away and you're protected, calm and satisfied with what you have.

3. "I'm a sad person," can change to, "I'm a happy person." This entire book speaks about it. You have to find happiness in yourself, you have to smile.

4. "I never smile being alone," is a easily solvable issue! Start doing it! Watch funny videos, write yourself a note that reminds you to smile and fake it till you make it!

5. "I often complain," can turn into, "I'm satisfied with my life." It's again a question of perception. It's about the devil that's not so black as he's painted. It's about the

rain that's not just wet but also refreshing and nurturing. It's about seeing the things in their true light and remembering that "realistic" isn't just negative! Positive is realistic, because negative complaining has never saved anyone nor improved a situation. Even if you want to get back money for a damaged purchase, you have a bigger chance to go away happy and satisfied if you explain the issue and ask for help in a positive manner. People love helping those who spread positivity, and your own brain will thank you by giving productive thoughts and positive solutions if you simply focus on positivity.

6. "I am a doubtful, suspicious person. I find it hard to trust new people and ideas," can change to, "I accept new people and ideas and I feel richly rewarded when others trust me." Work on reducing your doubtfulness and suspicion because it often makes you to say "no" to great opportunities. Doubt and suspicion come from fear, but fear can be reduced by becoming a self-confident person. Work on self-confidence to see and open the doors to new opportunities!

7. "I often feel stressed and anxious," can change to, "I'm calm and relaxed." The advice in statements 2 and 6 will help you here as well, and you'll enjoy a stress-free living.

8. "When I'm with others I usually don't show my emotions," can be, "I share my emotions with others and get the support I need." Nobody has the task of

guessing what happens inside of you. Hiding emotions can make you feel alone and separated from others, but friendships and close relationships are built of sharing those human moments—our emotions. Good relationships with others add to our feelings of happiness. If you don't hide grief and other emotions that make it harder to make it through the day, others can offer you a supporting shoulder when you need it. When you smile, others see you as an approachable, kind person. If you laugh when you want to, people will see you have a sense of humor and share laughs with you. Share your emotions, and your relationships will improve, making you more satisfied with what you have.

9. "When I'm with others usually my facial expression is serious, sad or neutral." If you have gotten so far in this book, you already know this statement isn't going to bring you closer to happiness. Many doors that lead to success and happiness are opened by smiles. Just try consciously putting a smile on your face in social situations and see how those situations change. People will share with you more warmth and kindness—isn't that also an important thing that can make us to feel good, appreciated and happy?

10. "I often see many obstacles and problems before I can see the successful result," may change to, "I acknowledge that my happiness depends only on me and I create obstacles that make me happy." It comes from you. Your happiness isn't created somewhere

outside and you're the only one who can make yourself happy. A smile that makes your body produce feel-good chemicals can make you to feel better. A smile that makes someone else see you as a friendly and nice person, trust in you and smile back.

11. "I don't laugh watching funny movies or hearing jokes," can change to, "I laugh when it's funny." Simply allow yourself to do it! Share your positive emotions letting them make you happier.

12. If you "do not fake smiling to create positive impression or make someone feel better," you know you what to do: fake it till you make it. Check the power of smile by faking it, and soon you won't be faking it any more—it'll become a part of you! You just have to try it a few times to see how your mindset changes because everything around you is changing.

13. "I often feel powerless and weak," probably happens to you precisely because of your negative mindset. It will naturally change to, "I feel strong and powerful," when you develop a positive mindset.

14. "I've never tried to use a smile to change any situation." You know what to do here. Try it! It's the key for making positive outcomes of almost any situation!

15. And if you fully agree with "I don't smile every day", remind yourself that it's important and you'll smile every day—just a bit more every day and step by step you'll move towards a new, much happier version of yourself.

By the way, check once again the answer you got to this question:

If you would summarize your persona in two lines, what would they be?

Do you still see it the same way or it has changed after taking this self-test? It doesn't have to change, but if it has changed you have probably opened to be a bit more honest with yourself than you were before. I actually hope you can see yourself in a more positive light now.

• What makes you happy?

A smile is a projection of happiness, and happiness is where natural smiles come from. We all want to be happy and many of us live in a seemingly endless search for happiness. A cake before bedtime, a million in the bank, Russian carpet on the wall or a diamond toilet seat. We're fooling ourselves with the thought that these things can bring happiness in our homes. In place of talking about what happiness is, I want to encourage you to find what makes you happy. Some things in life simply warm our hearts and put smiles on our faces. When you've found your positive vibe and integrated a positive mindset, you no longer have to push yourself to smile—it just happens: you smile while home alone, you share smiles with friends and strangers, you talk with a smile on your face and solve problems with it, and it comes back to you. Your life changes because instead of a piece of paper, your business card is your smile. A smile is the first thing people notice about you and it's what keeps you driven by positive brain chemistry. It's happiness that you have to let in.

I just want you to do one very simple thing: relax. Find some time for yourself. Put on some positive music that you enjoy, light candles if you like, but that's not obligatory, just make yourself comfortable and create an enjoyable environment around yourself. Silence can be very relaxing as well. If light exercising helps you to relax, do it. In fact, exercising is proven to release endorphins that relax the mind and the body. It does not matter what kind of physical activity you do. It may be walking for 15–30 min outside with ear buds and music or just listening to the wind and the birds. Activity will take your mind away from the negative moment and into a different moment of positive. If a cup of tea helps you to find your inner peace—make it for yourself. If you feel comfortable just the way you are right now, great—you're ready! Feeling comfortable will help you to find where your positive mindset is hiding. When you're relaxed and your mind is calm, simply take time for peaceful reflections and look for answers to these questions:

- What makes me to feel good?
- What are my happiest memories?
- What makes me feel at peace and harmonious with myself?
- What makes me feel good communicating with others?
- How can I share positivity with others to create more positive surroundings for myself?
- What can I do every day to make myself happier?

You don't necessarily have to find your final answers now, but try to find at least a few heart-warming memories or thoughts, a few things that make you to smile, at least a few actions you can take to make you happier. You can take notes and make lists of your happy things to keep them in your mind. What makes you happier isn't just thinking about happiness, but acting according to your happy thoughts. Don't ask yourself if you're happy or not! Allow yourself to be happy. Tell yourself that YOU ARE HAPPY.

Not just thinking about the beauty, magic and power of smile, but smiling itself is what makes the difference. Learn what makes you happy, develop a positive mindset, and discover your own potential to bring a change and smile. Smile for a change!

13

Unlock Your Smiling Hub

"Sometimes your joy is the source of your smile, but sometimes your smile can be the source of your joy."
–Thich Nhat Hanh, Buddhist monk,
author, and peace activist

My own belief in the enormous potential of changing lives by such a simple thing as a genuine smile comes from the journey of learning, observing, discovering and experimenting. No words could actually make you to understand the power of smiling better than experiencing it. As you know, the conscious mind is incredible—it's a passage through the critical factor and into our subconscious mind, where there is a direct connection to our memories and emotions and which is the core operator of our inner mind and inner body.

Instead of summarizing the entire book, to conclude, I want to give you a few new exercises and experiments that will help you unlock your "smiling hub." In giving you these experiments, I want to encourage you to check the power of your own smile and to reach your own conclusions. Nothing can convince the mind better than real experience and personal discoveries that you acknowledge through these experiences. I want you to see clearly the power of smiling in action—in your own life.

In this chapter you'll find practical exercises that'll help you to let the positive mindset pass through the gateway into your subconscious mind, unlocking your smiling genuineness and opening your mind to smiling more. The experiments given here aren't just for fun, although having fun, enjoying what you do and doing things with ease is important as well. This chapter is for you to bring out that genuine smile that carries beautiful and clear messages inside of you and outside—directed to the world around you. What goes around comes around! So, here are a few tips and experiments that will help you become aware of and use the power of smile.

Get comfortable with smiling

It might sound odd, but the world is full of people who really don't feel comfortable with smiling: they think they don't look good when smiling; they keep negative memories related to smiling; they simply aren't used to such emotional displays or this is how they have grown up—without sharing smiles.

Sometimes we forget to be happy or how to embrace happiness and we're caught in our own "life loop" that repeats, so we forget to stop, look and reevaluate what we do and what we may miss. If you still think that smiling makes you less attractive, read this book again! Smiling people ARE more attractive! They radiate good energy and attract it, they show that they're friendly and create trust, they're preferred for doing business with and have secret magnetism. Smiling people in general are MORE noticeable! If you see a picture with 50 people, and 10 of them are smiling, you'll be drawn to them first before noticing others. This is the power of smiling—it makes you likeable, forms connections with others and affects your mindset positively.

If you think your teeth are bad and it makes you too shy to smile, you might want to change the way of seeing yourself. Sometimes "bad teeth" are in the eye of the beholder; mostly it's a result of personal perception, not reality. You might think something is wrong with your teeth, although whatever you see as wrong is not as bad as refusing to smile. In many cases you will look MUCH better if you smile. Even if your teeth are not 100% shown while smiling, it's better than hiding your emotions and never sharing a smile. Imperfections don't make us less likeable, but desperately trying to hide them sends out the signal of you being uncomfortable and it doesn't create trust between you and others. There are many celebrities, singers, actors, politicians and entertainers who don't have perfect teeth, yet they smile in front of millions, and we like or love them. You can learn to smile in front of a mirror without showing all your teeth, check from which angles your smile looks better in pictures and draw attention to other features in your face, taking it away from your teeth, but remember that a genuine smile, genuine emotion you share with others dissolves what you might consider your flaws.

If you aren't comfortable with smiling because of traumatic past experiences, do yourself a favor—let that negativity go! I won't discuss more of it here, but, please, don't let negative past experiences define who you are now and shape your future. It's a general advice for everyone and in every situation: remember that your past experiences have shaped you, but you are not your past experiences. Put some efforts in learning to let go.

Finally, whatever is the reason that holds you back, you can get comfortable with smiling. You just need some practice:

- Allow yourself to smile while being alone. Smile watching funny videos and reading books, laugh watching comedy shows, crack a smile when you're being clumsy and so on—allow yourself to express your emotions when nobody is watching. There's no one judging you! Did a heart-warming or funny memory just popped-up in your mind? Smile! No, it's not odd—being alone we hug ourselves, dance in front of mirrors, play roles of different people and animals and talk to ourselves and objects around us. Smiling definitely doesn't make you weird. My father used to talk to himself all the time. I used to watch him sitting down and literally moving and nodding his head to agree or disagree with himself. It was a funny thing to see. He was just drifting away from the surroundings and sinking in a thought in his mind that he went over with himself. I remember the first time I saw it and went to him and said: "Hey, Dad, why are you nodding your head and who are you talking to?" He smiled and said: "I'm talking to myself!" I was surprised: "Yourself? Why? He replied, "I like to talk to smart people!" It brought a smile on my face and I remember laughing with him about it for years to come. Don't be ashamed to be who you are... smiles should be and might be a part of you!

- Get into activities that trigger smiling. Visit stand-up comedy show with your friends, listen to jokes, let the laughter out when it naturally comes—pamper yourself with activities that trigger smiling and laughing. Remember that one smile leads to another, and get this precious mechanism in motion! You can enjoy a good joke, sitcom or stand-up comedy show and have a blast. Being more open to humor will help you smile more often. It could also help to change your attitude—some small things in life really are more funny than tragic! Read a joke at least once or twice a day, find your favorite sitcom on TV... there are so many you will need to find time to sleep! YouTube is a great source of funny videos—from people to animals! Be open to comedy and laughter! In other words, laughter is the best medicine, and even when you feel better you want more of it... it's just like a good wine or a good meal, or a good movie that, when it ends, you want to see more.

- If you aren't comfortable sharing smiles because of your insecurities, you might need to work on your self-esteem—it often solves many problems in our lives! To connect with your smiling reflection, you can also use the "Smiling Eyes" exercise I described in Chapter #11: stand in front of a mirror, close your eyes, breathe deeply and imagine something positive—the best of your past or future vacation, smiles in faces of your grandchildren, your wedding day—it's up to you. Imagine what fills you with love and joy, put a smile on your face, charge this smile with positive energy and open your eyes. Simply look at your joyfully smiling face charged with positivity. Look into your own eyes, connect with your smiling reflection! That happy, smiling person—that's you!

This little exercise will help you accept your smiling reflection. As you engage in this exercise for a few days or weeks, you'll put in motion your positive mindset. If you like what you see in the mirror, your mind will make you smile more. It works the same way as with anything else in life: if you like having money, your mind pushes you to get more of it. If you enjoy chocolate cake, you will find the way to a café that serves it.

Observe to Understand

You can observe others and you can also pay attention to your own feelings in different situations. Observation is a very important part of learning. Kids learn very fast simply by observing what people around them are doing and how they're behaving. They learn by mimicking. As we grow up, we get information of how things work by simply observing them. To develop deep understanding of the role of a smile and make your mind accept how beneficial it is to smile more, use time in a social environment to observe people around you! At a party, social gathering, family dinner, bar, restaurant or any other place, when you sit with friends or family—observe how people are interacting with each other and how they interact with you. See how their facial expressions are changing. See who people are more attracted to—serious, grumpy people or those who are smiling and open for communication? Who you are more attracted to? Do you feel the same when communicating with grumpy and positive people? What's the difference? What kind of people make you smile? Observe to learn not just more about others, but about yourself and the power of smiling in action.

Test Your Smile

Test the knowledge you've gained in this book in different social situations and you will verify how your own smile works!

- Shopping experiment. A mall or a shopping street would be a perfect place for this experiment. Charge yourself with positivity, put a smile on your face and walk into a shop like a casual customer who is satisfied with life. Enjoy your shopping time and don't let the smile fade (remember, that you don't necessarily need a wide smile, smiling eyes will do the work as well and you can get them by a simple thought of being happy). You are here to check how smile changes communication with strangers! How do you feel being happy outside? Are other people smiling back to you, starting a conversation or getting involved in small talk with you? Do you feel better about yourself? Any change in the energy around you?

After happy-face shopping, go to another shop, but this time with a grumpy, serious face. Check what happens now? How fast are you approached? What facial expressions do you get back? How are people talking to you? Do people open up to you or keep a distance?

You will be surprised to see that smiling face is like a magnet. It makes people want to approach you faster, open a conversation with you and be closer to you.

- Happy family experiment. When talking to your life partner, kids, siblings or parents, see how communication changes if you're talking to them projecting happiness and smiling. When you talk to them projecting positive energy, they subconsciously perceive it. "Good morning!" can be said joyfully. "Goodbye," can be said with a smile on your face. Casual issues can be discussed while smiling, directions and tasks can be given with love and positive energy, and even educating your kids can be done while smiling making them to feel comfortable with you. Try it in your family!

- Say NO using a smile and polite, happy face. Saying "no" is hard, sometimes for both sides. It is not easy to express refusal or rejection as we usually do not want to hurt or upset the other side, or to push them away. However, from time to time you have to say it at work, to your employees or employers, or at home, to your spouse, kids or friends... Try saying "no" in a nice, soft voice and with smile in your face! There's a huge difference in how people perceive you when you are serious and when you are smiling. The same "no" becomes easier to accept because it's easier for us to accept people who are approaching us with friendliness. Saying "no" with a smiling kind face, adding a reason and a good feedback will always make a conversation smoother for both—you and the one you're talking to.

- Smile behind talking. If you talk while smiling you have better chances to be perceived with friendliness and trust, and if you ask for something there is a better chance you will really get it, but it's not just about big, shiny smiles. What matters the most is the feeling you're projecting and the tone of your voice while keeping a smile. Think about something that makes you happy (I hope, in the previous chapter you found what makes you happy) and ask, talk. You need to get that inner feeling of smiling and it'll get projected through you if it's inside of you. The happiness and spark of positivity doesn't always need a broad smile to be perceivable by others. It's in your eyes and your heart. When you talk with the inner feeling of smiling, you're warm and welcoming, friendly and trustworthy. You radiate true joy, and it makes you the person others want to see happy because you're sharing it. Is it easy to say "no" to a genuinely smiling child? Is it easy to walk away if you are addressed by a person who radiates genuine joy? Is it easy to refuse helping someone who is selflessly sharing happiness with others? It is easy only if your heart is made of pure ice, what isn't really possible... Try it! You can hide your physical smile, but if the right feeling is deep inside of your being, your whole body will project a smile.

If there is something that can bring positive change and only positive improvements in your life, this is it: your own smile. A day spent without smiling is empty. It depends only on you how fulfilled and happy your life is, so try these experiments to anchor in your mind a way to positively charged daily life. Observe, learn from your experiences, create those experiences and check how things work out in the presence of smile. Don't wait for someone to make you smile, but share a smile, use it and show the power of smile to others.

Project Smile

By the time you've arrived at the end of this book, I hope that it has helped you discover something, formulate in words what you already intuitively knew, and gain encouragement to work with yourself to instill a new perception in your own mind that makes your life positively charged.

If I could change the world for at least one day, my goal would be "Project Smile"—a day when everyone would smile and feel happy.

It's a day when no horror movies or thrillers, just comedy, romantic and happy dramas are broadcasted on TV.

It's a day when we say STOP to evil, and embrace kindness.

It's a day when we invite joy and push away negativity.

It's a day when we send out good energy and bring in even better one.

It's a day of love and passion.

It's a day where smiling is the #1 thing that comes to your face.

Just imagine: you can start the day with a genuinely positive mind. Problems aren't problems anymore because they aren't making your stress levels rise excessively. You embrace everything that's happening with joy. It's a day when you make a decision to be happy and everyone else does it too. We all decide to be happy, happy with our families and friends, happy at work, happy in our society. Simply and genuinely happy. When the day is started with a smile, it fulfills your heart and maps your day in a positive way, which can't be taken away from you by any obstacle or distraction. You decide to be happy and project it on people around you. They reflect your peaceful, joyful, harmonious happiness, and it spreads. Can you imagine it? That ease in your head and your entire body! That ease of happiness around you! When happy people come together, they can remove mountains, clean oceans, cross bridges and share kindness while enjoying being together. I can't imagine anything more beautiful than this.

That one full day of happiness, a project "Smile," is my dream project. You have probably heard this before: if you can imagine it, you can make it real. I can imagine that this day is really happening, bringing positive energy high above the sky. We thrive for happiness and positivity, so my prediction is that this wouldn't be just one day. It would go on.

I hope you'll join me in making it happen. So start with yourself. We only need to feel good to make ourselves and others feel better. Find the feeling of smiling inside of you and smile. The best moment to start is NOW. Don't wait for others to start; be the first, and others will join. Smiles will travel beyond you and reach others. Reach your neighbor, reach your city, state and country; your smile will travel oceans and reach the other side of the world. Imagine that even our enemies will smile for one day, smile from life and not smile from hate. Maybe this will manifest as peace in the world, and our peace of mind.

Let's embrace Project Smile and make it come one day.... every day!

Smile for confidence, success, prosperity and beautiful relationships.

Smile for a change in your life.

Smile for your own happiness.

Smile for a change in the world.

Smile for a change!

Afterword

*"The best time to plant a tree was 20 years ago. The
second best time is right now."*
–Ancient Chinese Proverb

A smile can change the moment, in fact, it can change your entire day and it may also change your life. There is a real, strong and beautiful life-changing power within a simple smile and it grows, spreads and multiplies whenever you chose to use it. The more you smile, the better you feel. The better you feel, the happier you become. The happier you become, the more people are drawn to you. The more people are drawn to you, the more loved and accepted you feel and more empowered you become. The more empowered you are, the more successful you become. The more successful you are, the more you are able to give back to others. The more you give back to others, the more fulfilled you will be. The more fulfilled you become, the more positive and happy you will be. You will be able to smile even more, and the more you will smile, the healthier you will be, and the healthier you will be, the longer and happier you will live. Smiling is a kick start to a whole new life, and an easy maintenance to your personal and social wellbeing. So, why not smiling? It is Free, it is Easy and it is so much fun!

Change starts with a decision, so, why don't you SMILE FOR A CHANGE?

"EVERY CHANGE STARTS WITH A DECISION."

CHOOSE TO SMILE!

–Guy Bavli

Thank you:

I would like to thank a few people who helped me along the way to make this book possible. First and foremost, to my beautiful wife Tal, who inspired and encouraged me to share my knowledge and passion with the world. Without her I would not be smiling as much.

To My kids: Shani, Roy and Eli, who make me a happy and proud dad. They bring a big smile to my face each day of my life. To my mother who has taught me the importance of a smile.

To My friends and workmates: Emily Hartstone, Julian Chagrin, and Rebecca Busch for your undeniable contribution to the making of the book. Lastly to Kristina, Elisabeth, Jorge, and Jason for making this book beautiful from the inside out.

References

1. Ekman, Paul (1993). "Facial expression and emotion" (PDF). *American Psychologist* 48 (4): 384–92. doi:10.1037/0003-066X.48.4.384. http://www.radford.edu/~jaspelme/_private/gradsoc_articles/facial%20expressions/Ekman%201993%20Am%20psych.pdf

2. Jack, Rachel E. (2010) "Cultural differences in the decoding and representation of facial expression signals." PhD thesis, University of Glasgow. http://theses.gla.ac.uk/2304/1/2010jackphd.pdf

3. Abel, E. L., & Kruger, M. L. (2010, Jan 26). Smile intensity in photographs predicts longevity. Psychological Science OnlineFirst, 21, 542–544. doi: 10.1177/0956797610363775 http://pss.sagepub.com/content/early/2010/02/26/0956797610363775.extract

4. Niedenthal Paula M., (2001) 15 (6), 853–864, "Cognition and Emotion" http://psych.wisc.edu/Brauer/BrauerLab/wp-

content/uploads/2014/07/Niedenthal-Brauer-
Halberstadt-Innes-Ker-2001-C_E.pdf

5. Henion Andy, Scott Brent (2011, Feb 22), "For a Better
    Work Day, Smile Like You Mean it", Michigan State
    University, retrieved from
    http://msutoday.msu.edu/news/2011/for-a-better-
    workday-smile-like-you-mean-it/

6. Kraft, Tara L. Pressman Sara D. (2012 Sep 24.), "Grin and
    bear it: the influence of manipulated facial expression
    on the stress response", 1372–8. doi:
    10.1177/0956797612445312.PubMed.gov
    http://www.ncbi.nlm.nih.gov/pubmed/23012270

7. Marianne LaFrance, Marvin A. Hecht, "Why Smiles
    Generate Leniency?", Boston College, Pers Soc Psychol
    Bull March 1995 vol. 21 no. 3 207–214, DOI:
    10.1177/0146167295213002
    http://psp.sagepub.com/content/21/3/207

8. Belinda Campos, Dominik Schoebi, Gian C. Gonzaga,
    Shelly L. Gable, Dacher Keltner. Attuned to the positive?
    Awareness and responsiveness to others' positive
    emotion experience and display. Motivation and
    Emotion, 2015; DOI: 10.1007/s11031-015-9494-x
    http://link.springer.com/article/10.1007%2Fs11031-
    015-9494-x